Instructor's Manual

Residential Mortgage Lending
Principles and Practices
Fifth Edition

Marshall W. Dennis
President, REMOC Associates, Ltd.

Thomas J. Pinkowish
President, Comunity Lending Associates

Prepared by

Marshall W. Dennis
President, REMOC Associates, Ltd.

THOMSON
SOUTH-WESTERN

Australia · Canada · Mexico · Singapore · Spain · United Kingdom · United States

Instructor's Manual For Residential Mortgage Lending, Principles and Practices, 5th Edition
Marshall W. Dennis

Vice President/ Editorial Director:
Jack Calhoun

Vice President/ Editor-in-Chief:
Dave Shaut

Sr. Acquisitions Editor:
Scott Person

Developmental Editor:
Sara Froelicher

Production Editor:
Jennifer Warner

Marketing Manager:
Mark Linton

Manufacturing Coordinator:
Charlene Taylor

Cover Design:
Bethany Casey

Printer:
Globus

TABLE OF CONTENTS

Chapter 1

History of Mortgage Lending

OVERVIEW OF CHAPTER

An historical perspective of mortgage lending is essential for an understanding of modern residential mortgage lending practices. This chapter explains the evolution of mortgage lending from the earliest beginnings through the Roman Era and the formative English period and finally through the American developments to present-day practices.

In this chapter the students will become aware of how the modern title and lien theories developed and how that development impacted the way mortgage lending was practiced by early mortgage lenders. The student will also be exposed to who the early mortgage lenders were and will come to understand their roles in providing financing for farmland and eventually individual homes.

A student will have difficulty understanding present-day residential mortgage lending without comprehending the impact of the major developments brought about by the Great Depression. The economic and political events of this period and the necessary steps at the federal level to alleviate the result of the Great Depression led to many innovative mortgage lending developments. These included the development of sound underwriting practices and the use of the long-term, self-amortizing mortgage loan. This period witnessed the involvement for the first time of the Federal Government in stimulating mortgage lending and eventually in regulating certain aspects of this important economic activity.

The end of World War II began an impressive period of growth for the entire economy, especially residential mortgage lending. Many returning servicemen took advantage of the *Servicemen's Readjustment Act* to obtain government guaranteed mortgage loans to purchase their first home. For the next couple of decades, residential mortgage lending grew rapidly and as a result so did Federal involvement including the creation of a new cabinet-level department called the Department of Housing and Urban Development (HUD).

As residential mortgage lending became an integral part of our society and its economic impact became more pronounced, a series of Federal regulations were enacted in the 1970s to ensure equality of opportunity in home ownership. These social and political changes produced a series of consumer protection laws such as *Equal Credit Opportunities Act*, *Truth in Lending*, and the *Real Estate Settlement Procedures Act*, among others.

Recent Residential Mortgage Lending

The financial problems of the 1980s are examined including deregulation, inflation, high interest rates, housing affordability issues and, finally, capital shortages. As the Federal Reserve attempted to address these problems, it found that some of the solutions had produced other negative events, such as the recession of the early 1980s. A casualty of these financial problems, especially high interest rates, coupled with poor management was the Savings and Loan (S & L) industry. The S & L failures produced such a loss to the insurance fund - FSLIC - that a federal bailout of nearly a half of trillion dollars was required.

The middle of the 1980s also witnessed a cyclical high for residential loan origination that was not to be duplicated until the early 1990s. Students should be made aware of the reasons for this cyclical high in originations and why it took another decade before those numbers are repeated. The principle reason for the nearly $450 billion in residential loan originations in 1986 - 87 was the continuing decline in interest rates from the highs of the early 1980s. This decline in interest rates was the primary reason that the percentage of refinancing to total loans originated increased from the normal twenty percent level to the forty percent point in both years.

The 1990s produced another period of boom for residential mortgage lending resulting in over $1 trillion of residential originations in 1993. This residential mortgage lending boom lasted well into the early 21st century with annual originations exceeding $2 trillion annually culminating with $3 trillion in originations in 2003. The same reason for the boom years of 2001-3 was 40 year lows in mortgage rates (reaching a low of 5.25 percent for a 30-year fixed-rate loan in early 2003).

OBJECTIVES OF CHAPTER

Upon successful completion of this chapter, students should be able to:

- Distinguish between title theory and lien theory.
- Describe the mortgage lending activities of the early thrifts, mortgage companies and commercial banks.
- Cite the effects of the Depression on financial institutions and their

mortgage lending practices.
- List and describe the function of the major federal legislation enacted to stabilize real estate values in the 1930s.
- Identify the reasons for the rapid growth in single-family mortgage lending after World War II.
- Identify the major consumer protection acts.
- Cite the impact of deregulation, inflation, and high interest rates and other recent events on the ability of the average American family to afford housing.
- Understand the magnitude of the refinancing wave of 2001-03 and how the average age of a 30-year mortgage loan was only about three years.

OUTLINE OF CHAPTER

I.   Ancient concepts of Mortgage Lending

    A.   Romans developed <u>Fiducia</u> (transfer)

    B.   <u>Hypotheca</u> (pledge) similar to modern lien theory

II.   English Developments

    A.   Lenders took title and possession in lieu of Interest

    B.   Courts of equity established favoring mortgagors

    C.   A balance reached - forerunner of modern title theory

III. American Developments

    A.   Real estate financing done by individuals

    B.   Temporary building associations forerunners of thrifts

    C.   Farms financed in Midwest and loans sold to East coast investors

    D.   Federally chartered commercial banks permitted to make real estate loans

    E.   Typical loan terms for early mortgages

    F.   Effects of Depression on real estate lending

IV.   Government Intervention

    A.   Federal government intervened in mortgage lending during Depression

    B.   Legislation to stabilize real estate values:

      1.   Reconstruction Finance Corporation Act (1932)

      2.   Federal Home Loan Bank Act (1932)

      3.   Homeowner's Loan Act (1933)

      4.   National Housing Act (1934)

V.   The Growth Era

    A.   Factors contributing to post—World War II housing boom

    B.   Creation of FHA and VA programs

VI.   Recent Mortgage Lending

    A.   Increased government involvement in secondary mortgage market

    B.   State Housing Agencies

    C.   Sale of tax-exempt bonds to finance housing

    D.   Consumer protection legislation

VII.   The Decade of Change

    A.   Problems: inflation, high interest rates, and capital shortages

    B.   Solutions: new sources of capital and alternative mortgage instruments.

    C.   Deregulation and the new rules of residential mortgage lending.

SUGGESTED TRUE/FALSE QUIZ

1.   Prior to the development of English common law, mortgage lending generally favored the mortgagor. **F**

2.   Under title theory, the title remains with the mortgagor, and the mortgagee has only a lien against the property. **F**

3.   In the U.S., little real estate financing was done on an organized basis until after the Civil War. **T**

4.   The first thrift institutions were created as temporary organizations, intended to exist only until each member purchased a home. **T**

5. Early mortgage companies primarily financed farms, and sold the loans to wealthy East coast investors. **T**

6. Commercial banks were originally organized to provide financing for farmland and homes. **F**

7. Amortization of mortgages was nonexistent before the 1930s. **T**

8. Following the stock market crash in 1929, lenders were able to sell foreclosed properties at inflated prices and earn record profits. **F**

9. Many states passed laws in the Depression years suspending foreclosures. **T**

10. The Federal Housing Administration (FHA) was created in the 1930s to purchase or refinance defaulted mortgages. **F**

11. Financial institutions suffered liquidity problems following World War II, due to the tremendous demand for housing by returning veterans. **F**

12. During the Great Depression mortgagors had little difficulty refinancing their home mortgage loans. **F**

13. Technology will continue to make mortgage originations easier for both borrower and lender. **T**

14. The creation of the secondary mortgage market contributed to a boom in housing construction and financing. **T**

15. Fannie Mae and Freddie Mac project that 13 to 15 million new households will be formed in the first decade of the new century. **T**

MULTIPLE CHOICE QUESTIONS. More than one answer may be correct – select all correct answers. (Correct answers are italicized.)

1. Under the feudal system in England the King was considered the owner of all land and allowed certain lords to use the land in return for:
   a. money
   b. *military service*
   c. friendship
   d. three cows and five sheep

2. The first financial institution formed for the purpose of financing the purchase of a house was:
   a. Mortgage companies
   b. Commercial banks
   c. ***Thrift institutions***
   d. Credit union

3. The typical mortgage loan at the turn of the century (1900) contained the following characteristics:
   a. maximum loan of 75 percent loan to value
   b. ***3 to 5 year term***
   c. *principal and interest paid semiannually*
   d. no refinancing option.

4. During the Great Depression mortgage lending suffered greatly including the following:
   a. ***27 states passed laws suspending foreclosure for a period of time***
   b. *20 percent of all mortgage assets were classified as "real estate owned"*
   c. states giving land away to displaced farmers
   d. federal government allowed homeowners to stay in home.

5. The Federal Government took a leading role in mortgage lending <u>during</u> the Great Depression by enacting the following legislation:
   a. Servicemen's Readjustment Act
   b. Real Estate Settlement Procedures Act (RESPA)
   c. ***National Housing Act***
   d. *Home Owners Loan Act*

SUGGESTED SHORT ESSAY QUESTIONS

1. Describe the underwriting standards and mortgage loan terms that prevailed in the 1920s. How did they contribute to the high foreclosure rates in the 1930s?

   <u>ANSWER:</u> As real estate values appreciated sharply, lenders became careless about underwriting standards and made many imprudent loans. Workers lost their jobs, were unable to make the quarterly or semiannual interest payments, and as a result lost their property. Even those homeowners who retained their jobs were often the victims of foreclosure. The reason for this was that mortgages at this time had only a three to five year term and since they were not amortized they had to be paid off or renewed. As savers withdrew their funds from all financial institutions, most of these institutions had no money to lend, and thus the borrowers who had to refinance their loan at the end of the term often lost their property.

2.   How were the same financial institutions, which suffered a liquidity crisis and huge losses in the 1930s able to accommodate the demand for housing at the end of World War II?

ANSWER: During World War II financial institutions invested huge amounts of assets in no-risk, low yielding war bonds. At the end of the war these bonds were sold and the cash converted into higher yielding mortgage loans. Another important factor was that a higher proportion of an institution's assets could be invested, since many loans were either insured by FHA or guaranteed under the *Servicemen's Readjustment Act*.

3.   Describe the conditions that were conducive to $2 and $3 trillion being originated in the early part of the 21st century.

ANSWER: After the cyclical high interest rates of the early 1980s, interest rates began a long slide allowing long-term interest rates to hit a 40-year low in 2003. Rates for a 30-year mortgage declined from approximately 18 percent in 1982 to as low as 5.25 percent twenty years later. Much of the decline in rates after the stock market decline in 2001 and resulting recession was the result of the Federal Reserve dropping the feds fund target rate 13 times over a two-year period.   During this period homeownership reached 68 percent – the highest ever.

ANSWERS TO ORAL DISCUSSION POINTS

The discussion points at the end of each chapter are intended for oral discussion in class. Suggested answers/points to emphasize for the questions are found below.

1.   Examine how the concept of private ownership of land has evolved since the days of the Egyptians.

ANSWER: Ownership of land has always been an important part of law and commerce even as early as the days of the early Egyptians and Babylonians. Hand in hand with ownership of land went using land as security for debt. Complete ownership of land is a reality that probably will never occur but increased ownership of land by individuals has been an historical development from the earliest times and in particular during the development of the English Common Law. The feudal system of land tenure ushered in the concept of inheritable interests in land. Finally, the development of American Law brought great ownership in law for the individual.

2.   How has the involvement of the federal government in real estate and mortgage lending allowed for growth in homeownership?

ANSWER: Although the Federal Government was reluctant to get involved in real estate for many decades, the Great Depression changed that position. Since that period the Federal Government has been involved in developing new ways of financing homes (long-term, fully amortized loans), provided Federal Government insurance and guarantees for loans (FHA and VA) and recently has enacted many laws and regulations to ensure the equal treatment of all people in getting mortgage loans. Additional involvement of the Federal Government has been in starting a secondary mortgage market and enacting laws governing the mortgage transaction (RESPA, etc).

3.   The Great Depression was the beginning of modern residential mortgage lending. Examine the changes that occurred during this period and their importance to modern mortgage lending

ANSWER: The Great Depression was so severe that the Federal Government understood it must get involved or the entire economy and maybe the type of government would be changed. The enactment of federal insurance on deposits brought money back into the financial institutions. These funds could be loaned to individuals for mortgage loans because the loans were backed by Federal insurance. FHA also introduced the concept of a long-term, self-amortizing mortgage loan.

4.   The 1960-1970 period witnessed the enactment of many major consumer protection laws/regulations. How have these federal enactments changed the way residential mortgage lending is conducted?

ANSWER: The primary focus of Federal involvement was in stimulating the economy and in protecting the rights of groups of individuals who had been denied credit in the past. These groups included women, racial minorities, and people who had recently arrived in this country. Federal laws also helped to keep the cost of borrowing down with the passage of TIL, Real Estate Settlements Procedures Act, etc.

5.   What is the difference between the *Title Theory* and *Lien Theory* of mortgage lending? Which exists in your state?

ANSWER: Title theory was developed by English courts of equity in the 1600s in an effort to balance the rights of mortgagors and mortgagees. Under title theory, the mortgagor retains possession of the property, but relinquishes title to the mortgagee. When the debt is repaid, the title is reconveyed to the borrower. Under lien theory, the mortgagor retains both possession and title to the property. However, the mortgagee has a legal claim against the property. If the debt is not satisfied, the mortgagee may take possession of, and title to, the property. In the second part of the question, students should identify the procedure used in their own states. The instructor should verify which theory is followed within their state.

CHAPTER 2

ROLE OF MORTGAGE LENDING

IN THE ECONOMY

OVERVIEW OF THE CHAPTER

This chapter is designed to help students understand the importance of housing and mortgage lending to the entire American economy. This is accomplished by first explaining how changes in the economy affect savings inflows, capital formation, and eventually, mortgage lending. The users of credit are identified and the impact of government borrowing on the financial markets is examined. The distinctions between roles of financial intermediaries, mortgage lenders and mortgage investors are described.

The Federal Reserve's important role in managing the economy is described and emphasis is placed on the "Feds" attempt to stabilize economic forces by controlling the supply of money. Probably the best example in recent history of the Feds attempt to stabilize the economy can be seen in the 13 changes in the fed funds rate between 2000 and 2003. The result was a fed funds rate of 1 percent and a prime rate of 4.25 percent in 2003. The resulting 40-year low in long-term mortgage rates produced a record year of originations in 2002-03. These record years probably will not be repeated for many years. The chapter ends with a discussion of some of the recent trends in residential mortgage lending.

SPECIAL NOTES - Idea for classroom discussion:

The rate of savings in the United States has been declining steadily since the early 1970s but it appears that the decline has ended - at least for the moment. The latest figures place the savings rate at about 2.4 percent (end of 2002) of disposable income. This modest number - a slight increase from a couple of years ago - is clearly the result of increased caution on the part of the average consumer as the direct result of the events of 9/11 and the stock market decline. Although there has been a modest increase, the current amount of savings is not sufficient to meet the capital formation needs of this country.

After World War II and well into the 1970s, the U.S. was able to meet its capital formation needs with a savings rate around 8 percent. Today, as mentioned, the U.S. is far from that rate. This decrease in the savings rate is even more damaging with the dramatically increased borrowing needs of the federal government in the early part of the new century. **The federal debt changed rapidly from a surplus in 2001 to an expected deficit of nearly $500 billion in 2004.** The result of this imbalance has been the shifting of the status of the U.S. from being the largest creditor nation in the world to being the largest debtor nation. Just the interest payments on this amount of debt and the resulting higher interest rates will have a strongly negative impact on the U.S. economy and, of course, on residential mortgage lending. Instructors may want to discuss with their students what is being done to correct this imbalance.

OBJECTIVES OF CHAPTER

Upon successful completion of this chapter, students should be able to:

- Explain how changes in the business cycle affect real estate sales activity and mortgage lending.
- Cite the impact of the government's deficit spending on interest rates and the supply of capital.
- Identify three ways the Federal Reserve exercises monetary control
- Compare and contrast the functions of financial intermediaries, mortgage lenders, and mortgage investors.
- Explain why Money Market Certificates (MMCs) failed to correct the problem brought about by inflation and excessive credit demand.

OUTLINE OF CHAPTER

I.   Capital Formation

    A.   Importance of individual saver

    B.   Influences on savings inflows

    C.   Cause and effect of disintermediation

    D.   Countercyclical nature of real estate activity

II.   Mortgage Markets

    A.   Competition for funds in capital market

B.   Interest rate determinants

III.   Public Debt vs. Private Debt

IV.   Federal Reserve Credit Control

    A.   Reserve requirements

    B.   Open market operations

    C.   Discount rate

V.   Financial Intermediaries

    A.   Function

    B.   Investment alternatives

VI.   Mortgage Lenders

    A.   Lend funds directly to borrowers

    B.   Purchase mortgages originated by others

    C.   Originate residential and income—property loans

VII   Mortgage investors

    A.   Important holders of mortgage debt

    B.   Usually do not originate mortgage loans

VIII. Trends in Mortgage Lending

    A.   Inflation and volatile interest rates

    B.   Disintermediation and shortage of funds

    C.   Earnings problem

    D.   Traditional savings and mortgage instruments not viable

IX.   Money Market Certificates

    A.   Issued to stem outflow of funds

    B.   Caused mortgage rates to stay higher longer

SUGGESTED TRUE/FALSE QUIZ

1.   Savings of individuals make up an insignificant part of the funds required by the financial market. **F**

2. Mortgage lending is part of the capital market. **T**

3. Housing and related sectors account for less than 10 percent of gross domestic product. **F**

4. As a general rule, financial intermediaries can earn higher yields on investments than individuals can. **T**

5. Money market certificates (MMCs) have increased savings inflows to banks and thrifts. **T**

6. The Federal Reserve is responsible for fiscal and monetary control. **F**

7. Low interest rates usually do not stimulate the housing market because too many people are out of work. **F**

8. The primary risk to portfolio lenders is interest rate risk. **T**

9. The term financial intermediary refers to the person who is a middle man between financial institutions. **F**

10. The value of all homes in the U.S. is approximately $12 trillion. **T**

MULTIPLE CHOICE QUESTIONS. More than one answer may be correct – select all correct answers. (Correct answers are italicized.)

1. Disintermediation usually occurs under the following circumstances <u>except</u> when:
   a. demand for credit is high.
   b. the economy expands.
   c. interest rates are high.
   d. *interest rates are low.*

2. Real estate activity and mortgage lending usually expand when the
   a. *demand for credit is low.*
   b. demand for credit is high.
   c. business cycle is at its peak.
   d. interest rates are high.

3.   Increased borrowing by the government results in all of the following except:
     a.   lower interest rates.
     b.   higher interest rates.
     c.   inflation
     d.   increased competition for funds.

4.   When the Federal Reserve buys securities and issues a check drawn upon itself, which method of credit control is it exercising?
     a.   It is decreasing the supply of money by discounting commercial paper.
     b.   It is increasing the supply of money through open market operations.
     c.   It is decreasing the supply of money through open market operations.
     d.   It is increasing the supply of money by lowering reserve requirements.

5.   Which of the following is not an example of a mortgage lender?
     a.   Commercial bank
     b.   Life Insurance company
     c.   Retirement and pension fund
     d.   Credit Union

SUGGESTED SHORT ESSAY QUESTIONS

1.   If demand for funds is high, and corporate bonds offer the same rate as mortgages, funds will generally flow to bonds. Explain why this is true, and what actions mortgage lenders can take to ease this problem.

     ANSWER: Mortgage loans are less attractive to investors because they lack uniformity, are less liquid, and can be "tied up" in lengthy foreclosures. Lenders can ease this problem by using: (a) improved underwriting policies and procedures, (b) uniform documentation, (c) improved appraisal procedures. Shorter-term mortgages and balloon payments may be appropriate in some situations since they tend to increase liquidity. If this is not feasible, lenders may increase portfolio yields by including adjustable rate mortgages with short-term indices. Lenders must also work with the courts and lawmakers to improve and update the foreclosure process.

2.   Why is mortgage lending impacted negatively by excessive governmental borrowing?

     ANSWER: The key ingredient for high mortgage lending activity is the interest rate. The interest rate is established by the demand for funds. The supply of funds is limited, therefore if the demand increases, the cost of money, as measured by the interest rate, will increase. As a result fewer families will be able to qualify at the increased interest rate and thus will not be able to afford the median priced home. This result was witnessed during the early part of the 1980s, which resulted in lowered originations.

ANSWERS TO ORAL DISCUSSION POINTS

The discussion points at the end of each chapter are intended for oral discussion in class. Suggested answers/points to emphasize for the questions are found below.

1.   Real estate and mortgage lending are a major part of the American economy. Examine and explain the magnitude of their involvement in the economy.

<u>**ANSWER:**</u> Economists have concluded that housing and related sectors account for about 21 percent of the Gross Domestic Product (GDP) - a measure of the nation's total output of goods and services. Examples of the economic importance of housing, and therefore residential mortgage financing, comes from the **National Association of Home Builders (NAHB, www.nahb.com)** which estimates that housing construction, sales and financing account for one out of every twelve jobs in the United States. The NAHB calculated in 2002 that the economic impact of the construction of 1,000 single-family houses created nearly 1,800 man-years of employment and over $80 million in wages and more than $42 million in federal, state and local tax revenues. This economic stimulus was then and is now vital for a strong national economy.

2.   Real estate and mortgage lending are significantly impacted by changes in the economy, especially interest rates.   What was the impact on mortgage lending of the dramatic drop in interest rates in 2001-02? Why did interest rates drop so much?

<u>**ANSWER:**</u> The low interest rates during this period (30-year rates reached a low of 5.75 in 2002) allowed record originations of over $2 trillion in 2002. These low interest rates allowed more people to become homeowners as witnessed by the homeownership rate, which reached an all-time high of 68 percent in that same year. Low rates also allowed these homebuyers to purchase more expensive homes than they might otherwise have been able to afford. The ability of the Federal Reserve to influence the economy was very evident during the first two years of the new century. During 2001 and 2002, the Federal Reserve cut the Fed Funds target rate twelve times trying to stimulate the economy slowed by the twin forces of recession and the terrorist

attack of September 11, 2001.

3. What is the difference between financial intermediaries, mortgage lenders and mortgage investors?

   ANSWER: The more modern and clearly more descriptive term, **financial intermediaries**, describes that classification of economic units that previously were called financial institutions. Their principal economic function is to serve as the middleman - the intermediary - between the saver and the borrower. Both saver and borrower benefit from this arrangement. The primary economic function of a residential **mortgage lender** is to lend money for the purchase or refinancing of residences of all types in the primary mortgage market. These loans are often sold to **investors** who acquire the mortgage debt they hold either directly from the mortgage lenders that originated them or through the operation of the secondary mortgage market.

4. How does the "Fed" attempt to manage the economy? What tools are most important?

   ANSWER: An important element in determining interest rates is monetary policy. Monetary policy (as controlled by the Federal Reserve) occurs when the supply of money is controlled rather than interest rates. Thus, if the Federal Reserve wants to stimulate the economy, it would increase the supply of money. The fiscal policy of the federal government often forces the Federal Reserve to act in an attempt to moderate the impact of federal borrowing on the nation's economy. Important tools are: **Reserve requirements.** By increasing the amount of money a member institution must have in its reserve account, less money is available to be loaned; **Open-market operations.** This commonly used method allows the Federal Reserve to decrease the supply of money by selling treasury securities on the open market; **Fed Funds Target – Intended Federal Funds Rate.** Open market operations (purchases and sales of U.S. Treasury and federal agency securities) are the Federal Reserve's principal tool for implementing monetary policy; Discount **rate.** The Federal Reserve operates a service of discounting (paying less than par) commercial paper from member institutions.

5. As a general rule, from where does the money for residential mortgage lending come?

   ANSWER: The funds required for capital formation are derived primarily from the savings of individuals and businesses. This process of capital formation produces most of the capital used by the various segments of our economy. They exceed personal savings by a substantial amount. However, the savings generated by individuals - either as deposits at financial institutions or as reserves in whole life insurance policies - account for approximately 90 percent of the funds used for residential mortgage lending.

6. How do demographic forces impact real estate and the mortgage markets?

   ANSWER: Demographic forces are contributing to continued strength in housing demand. Couples reaching their home buying years, new immigrants and certain minority groups are creating demand for housing. These groups are forming new households at an annual rate of more than 1 million per year. This rate of growth in new households is expected to continue for the next decade. Financing this demand for housing will challenge the housing finance system but will also provide an opportunity for tremendous growth in residential mortgage lending for mortgage lenders.

CHAPTER 3

THE MORTGAGE LENDERS

OVERVIEW OF CHAPTER

This chapter describes those mortgage lenders that are currently involved in originating residential mortgage loans. These lenders include mortgage bankers and mortgage brokers, commercial banks, savings and loan associations, savings banks, and credit unions. The historical development, organization, and regulation of these lenders are described, along with a comparison of their sources of funds and any interdependent relationship is revealed. The description of the varying activities and investment philosophies of these lenders shows that each has a unique place in today's mortgage market.

Another historic change in residential mortgage lending over the past couple of years has been an increase in the percentage of loans originated by the top twenty-five lenders. In prior years residential mortgage lending was very local in focus. Few regional lenders existed and no true national mortgage lenders had developed. Until recently, no mortgage lender had ever originated even one percent of the total national mortgage originations. In 1986 this all changed, probably forever. In that year, Citicorp (and its' subsidiaries) originated over three percent of the record total originations for that year. In 2001 the dominance of the larger lenders became even more evident as the top five originators originated 38 percent of all 1-4 family mortgage debt. That, in an industry that had over 10,000 lenders.

OBJECTIVES OF CHAPTER

Upon successful completion of this chapter, students should be able to:

- Explain which mortgage lenders are most important in residential mortgage lending as originators and which are investors.
- Explain how actions taken by the federal government aided in the development of the various residential mortgage lenders.
- Identify the sources of funds for each of the lenders.

- Compare and contrast the activities and investment philosophies of the various lenders.
- Describe how commercial banks, mortgage companies and the two thrifts are organized and regulated.
- Explain why credit unions believe they must get involved in residential mortgage lending.

OUTLINE OF CHAPTER

I. Mortgage Bankers (MB)

    A. Characteristics

        1. Financial intermediary, but not depository

        2. Move funds from capital-surplus to capital-short areas

        3. Lead in originating FHA/VA mortgages

    B. Development

        1. Originally financed farms and sold mortgages to investors

        2. Single-family mortgages first made after WW I

        3. Servicing of FHA loans changes business

        4. Originated FHA/VA after WW II

    C. Organization and Regulation

        1. Governed by state partnership or incorporation laws

        2. Audited by HUD

    D. Financing the MB

        1. Lending activity financed by sale of commercial paper or warehouse lines of credit

        2. Source of revenue

    E. MB Today

        1. Servicing of loans for others

        2. Selected ratios

II. Commercial Bank

A.   Characteristics

    1.   Largest in membership and assets

    2.   Leads in origination of income property loans

B.   Development

    1.   State-chartered banks were making real estate loans fifty years before national banks

    2.   FDIC created in 1933

C.   Organization and regulation

    1.   Dual charter system

    2.   Federal Reserve System

D.   Mortgage lending activity

    1.   Deposits and loans generally short-term

    2.   Commercial loans favored over mortgage loans

    3.   Active in construction lending

    4.   Lending terms and limits regulated by Feds and states

    5.   Recent expansion of residential mortgage lending

III.   Savings Institutions

A.   Savings and Loans (S&Ls)

    1.   Number of S&Ls peaked in 1929

    2.   Half failed in 1930s

    3.   Numbers are now about 1,000

B.   An Institution in Trouble

    1.   The problems of the 1980s

    2.   FIRREA – end of an era

C.   Organization and Regulation

    1.   May be state or federally chartered

    2.   May be mutual or stock association

    3.   Federal S&Ls must belong to FHLB and FSLIC

D.   Mortgage Lending Characteristics

        1.   Largest holder of residential mortgage debt

        2.   Historically local lender

        3.   Entry into secondary mortgage market in 1975

        4.   Emphasis on conventional loans

        5.   Lending limits and powers

IV.   Savings Banks

    A.   Development

        1.   Historical development similar to S&Ls

        2.   Never spread far from eastern part of country

    B.   Organization and Regulation

        1.   Originally all were mutual but now about 40% are stock.

        2.   Members of FDIC

    C.   Mortgage Lending Activity

        1.   Have greater experience making other types of loans in addition to residential mortgages

        2.   In general, have been more profitable then S&Ls

V.   Credit Unions

    A.   Development

        1.   One of the fastest—growing financial institutions

        2.   High number of members

    B.   Mortgage Lending Activity

        1.   Forced into mortgage lending by change in competition in consumer lending

        2.   Rapid increase in mortgage lending activity

SUGGESTED SHORT ANSWER QUIZ (Replaces T/F for this chapter)

Directions: Fill In **"CB"** if the statement applies to a commercial bank, **"MC"** if it applies to a mortgage company, **"T"** if it applies to thrifts, and **"CU"** if it applies to a credit union.

1. The type of financial institution that is the largest holder of residential mortgage debt. **T**

2. This mortgage lender is a financial intermediary, but not a depository. **MC**

3. About 50 - 60 percent of each year's residential originations are made by this lender. **MC**

4. Its deposits and loans are generally short-term. **CB**

5. Purchasers of mortgages or insuring/ guaranteeing agencies impose the only restrictions on residential mortgage lending for this lender. **MC**

6. Is the largest originator of FHA/VA loans each year. **MC**

7. This lender is limited as to whom it can grant a mortgage loan. **CU**

8. It is the largest of all mortgage lenders in number of institutions <u>and</u> assets. **CB**

9. This lender borrows money to lend on mortgages by selling commercial paper, mortgage loans or warehousing mortgages. **MC**

10. This classification of mortgage lender leads all mortgage lenders in originating conventional loans. **T**

11. This lender is only directly supervised by HUD. **MC**

12. Although this lender is a major mortgage lender, it must borrow money to lend. **MC**

13. It is the financial institution that provides much of the funds used by mortgage bankers. **CB**

14. It has only recently become a meaningful originator of residential mortgage loans. **CU**

15. It was forced into mortgage lending by a change in the competition in consumer lending. **CU**

MULTIPLE CHOICE QUESTIONS. More than one answer may be correct – select all correct answers. (Correct answers are italicized.)

1. Which organization insures the deposits of commercial banks and savings?
   a. Office of Thrift Supervision
   b. Savings Insurance Fund
   c. Federal National Mortgage Insurance
   d. Federal Deposit Insurance Corporation

2. Which of the following mortgage lenders is not a depository institution?
   a. Savings Banks
   b. Credit Unions
   c. Mortgage Banker
   d. Commercial Banks

3. Name the mortgage lender that typically specializes in construction loans:
   a. Thrifts
   b. Commercial Banks
   c. Credit Unions
   d. Mortgage Banker

4. This lender can only make mortgage loans to a specified group of people:
   a. Commercial Bank
   b. Mortgage Banker
   c. Thrifts
   d. Credit Union

5. This lender typically originates over half of all residential loans each year:
   a. Credit Union
   b. Commercial Bank
   c. Thrift
   d. Mortgage Banker

SUGGESTED SHORT ESSAY QUESTIONS.

1. Give an example of how the federal government aided in the development of

each of the following mortgage lenders: federally-chartered commercial banks, and mortgage companies.

ANSWER: Commercial banks: students may list either the Federal Reserve Act, passed in 1913, which permitted federally- chartered banks to make mortgage loans; or the Banking Act of 1933, which included creation of the FDIC. The FDIC Insurance protection helped lure funds for new loans back into banks.

Mortgage companies: students may list the HOLC created in 1933, which permitted lenders to exchange defaulted mortgages for government bonds, or FHA- insured and VA-guaranteed loans that became the mainstay of mortgage companies.

2. Explain why mortgage companies depend on commercial banks as a source of funds.

ANSWER: Mortgage companies are not depository institutions. Mortgage companies must use closed loans as collateral and draw on a line of credit at a commercial bank to finance their lending, unless conditions are right for selling commercial paper. Even the latter may require bank backing and compensating funds on deposit with a commercial bank.

3. Commercial banks, mortgage companies and thrifts originated many kinds of mortgage loans, but each one specializes in a particular type of residential loan. Identify each mortgage lender's specialty, and explain the reason behind each lender's choice.

ANSWER: Commercial banks lead in construction loans, because banks' deposits are generally short-term. They prefer short-term loans but are becoming meaningful originators of long-term loans also.
Mortgage companies originate 75 percent of all FHA-VA mortgages. These lenders do not wish to hold the mortgages, but seek readily saleable loans for investors, the secondary market, or GNMA mortgage-backed securities.

Thrifts (both S & Ls and Savings Banks) are most interested in originating conventional loans and engaging in local lending. In prior years much of this activity was placed in portfolio of thrifts but today most loans from these lenders are sold in the secondary mortgage market.

ANSWERS TO ORAL DISCUSSION POINTS

The discussion points at the end of each chapter are intended for oral discussion in class. Suggested answers/points to emphasize for the questions are found below.

1.   Explain which mortgage lenders are most important in residential mortgage lending as originators and which as investors.

       ANSWER: Mortgage brokers and mortgage bankers are important as originators but do not invest in mortgages. Commercial banks both originate and invest in residential mortgage loans. Thrifts both originate and hold a substantial amount of residential mortgage loans. Credit unions both originate and hold residential mortgage loans.

2.   Examine and explain the major difference between mortgage brokers/bankers and portfolio lenders.

       ANSWER: Unlike other mortgage lenders, a mortgage banker does not intentionally hold mortgages for its own benefit. Since a mortgage banker does not have a traditional portfolio like other intermediaries, all residential mortgage loans are originated with the intent of selling the loans to mortgage investors either directly or through the secondary mortgage market. On occasion, a mortgage banker may originate a "mistake" which cannot be sold as a conforming loan to an established investor. When this happens, the mortgage banker will usually sell the loan to another investor at a discount rather than hold on to it.

3.   The mortgage broker is a major originator of residential mortgages. Explore the inherent conflict a mortgage broker faces when originating a mortgage loan.

       ANSWER: Mortgage brokers typically charge fees to the mortgage applicant and also receive fees from a wholesale lender. Is this legal? RESPA allows fees to be charged by service providers, as long as those fees are reasonable for services, goods, or facilities actually provided. Similar to retail mortgage originators (like commercial banks or mortgage banks), mortgage brokers provide the same services to consumers for which an origination fee is often charged. These loan origination services include: taking the loan application, ordering the credit report and appraisal, counseling the consumer on the loan process, and collecting the necessary documents. Mortgage brokers may also receive a fee from the wholesale purchaser. This fee is earned because the broker provides separate and distinct services to wholesale lenders. These include marketing the lender's products and assembling and delivering the completed loan package. In addition to a fee for these services, wholesale lenders may pay mortgage brokers a premium, ("yield spread premium" or "service release premium"), which may include compensation for the services and facilities, but also represents payment for the intrinsic market value of the closed loan.

4.   Why are mortgage bankers tied so closely to commercial banks?

ANSWER: An alternative used by mortgage bankers to obtaining funds to be loaned to residential mortgagors is by drawing on a line of credit with a commercial bank. This process is usually a part of a unique function performed by mortgage bankers - warehousing. Warehousing refers to the function of mortgage bankers holding mortgages in the "warehouse" on a short-term basis pending sale to an investor. These first mortgage loans held in the warehouse also serve as security for the revolving line of credit at a commercial bank. This process finances the mortgage banker's loans to borrowers and the mortgage banker's inventory of closed residential loans. The loan from the commercial bank will require that it be fully collateralized by closed mortgage loans retained by the mortgage banker until enough loans are grouped for sale to investors

5. Which mortgage lender originates the majority of FHA/VA mortgage loans? Why is this the case?

ANSWER: Mortgage bankers originate nearly 75 percent of yearly originations of FHA/VA loans. The primary reason for this dominant position is the desire of mortgage bankers to increase their FHA/VA servicing that can generate as much as 40 basis points per loan serviced.

CHAPTER 4

STRATEGIES FOR GENERATING

RESIDENTIAL LOANS

OVERVIEW OF CHAPTER

For fifty years after the Great Depression, residential mortgage loan origination was primarily a local activity. That is, local financial institutions originated the vast majority of mortgage loans in that local market place. As discussed previously, this is a situation that is changing rapidly in many areas of the country today as large, national concerns begin to dominate local market places. As a result of this change and others, which impact how mortgages are originated, the methodology of loan origination has taken on greater importance and thus the reason for this chapter.

The first part of this chapter deals with getting an applicant in the door and with helping originators understand the natural apprehension that applicants feel when applying for a mortgage loan. The second part deals with the mechanics of originating loans and with the two major approaches to origination – retail and wholesale.

An important discussion that should occur in class is why did originations decline to the extent they did in the mid-1990s from the record highs of 1992-93? At the time this instructor's manual was being written, it appears that originations for 2003 are going to be in the $3 trillion range or a slight increase over the record year of 2002. Students should understand the negative impact the increase in interest rates had on originations over the second half of 2003. The impact was two-pronged: first, as interests increased, fewer people could qualify for a mortgage loan; and second, as rates stabilized or increased slightly, consumers were no longer interested in refinancing their mortgages. During 2002 and the firs half of 2003, it is estimated that about seventy percent of the origination activity was the result of refinancing, a dramatic increase from the more normal thirty percent.

OBJECTIVES OF CHAPTER

Upon successful completion of this chapter, students should be able to;

- Identify the requirements for successful mortgage lending
- Describe the importance of the origination function and what it consists of
- Explain the reasons for some of the recent developments in serving the public in the requests for mortgage loans
- Identify those attributes which attract customers to mortgage lenders
- Distinguish between the retail and wholesale methods of loan origination
- Explain the advantages and disadvantages of the retail and wholesale methods
- Understand some of the expenses associated with the origination function.

OUTLINE OF CHAPTER

E.   Retail branch office

IV.   Wholesale Loan Origination

    A.   Reasons for the development of wholesale mortgage lending

    B.   Different fee structure than retail

V.   Advantages and Disadvantages of Wholesale Lending

    A.   Number of loans produced

    B.   Ability to move quickly

    C.   Issue of quality control

SUGGESTED TRUE/FALSE QUIZ

1.   In today's market place, all a lender has to do is advertise that it is offering mortgages and it will get all of the business it can handle. **F**

2.   The largest originator of residential mortgages over the past couple of years was thrifts. **F**

3.   The realtor is considered among the most important factors in a borrowers   selection of a mortgage lender. **T**

4.   The retail method of loan origination is the traditional method familiar to most borrowers. **T**

5.   A commissioned loan agent generally earns a 50 basis points commission. **T**

6.   Loan demand is driven more by demographic issues than interest rates. **F**

7.   The average percentage of yearly originations that are refinancing is about 50 percent. **F**

8.   One point equals one percent of the mortgage amount. **T**

9.   Table funding occurs when a broker closes a mortgage loan with funds belonging to an acquiring lender. **T**

10.   Yield spread premiums are illegal under RESPA. **F**

SUGGESTED MULTIPLE CHOICE QUESTIONS. More than one answer may be correct, select all that are correct. (Correct answers are italicized.)

1. For any residential mortgage lender to be successful, certain elements must be in place including:
    a.   *Loan demand*
    b.   *Trained personnel*
    c.   *Product Offerings*
    d.   Public image

2. The highest loan origination volume in U.S. history is:
    a. $1 trillion
    b. $2 trillion
    c.   *$3 trillion*
    4. $4 trillion

3. Variable-rate first mortgage loan (ARMs) originations vary depending on interest rates. The highest percent of total year originations for ARMs was:
    a.   20 percent
    b.   30 percent
    c.   40 percent
    d.   *70 percent*

4. According to the Mortgage Bankers Association, the three most important factors in attracting consumers are:
    a.   *Low interest rates*
    b.   Convenience of home application
    c.   *Referral by real estate agent*
    d.   *Company reputation*

5. In today's evolving primary mortgage market, the four strategies or methods of origination include:
    a.   *Retail origination*
    b.   *Wholesale origination*
    c.   International origination
    d.   Real estate agent origination

SUGGESTED SHORT ESSAY QUESTIONS

1. Discuss the impact FASB #91 has on the pricing of residential mortgage loans.

   ANSWER: The students should understand what FASB #91 requires and also that the requirements will lessen the attractiveness of "point lending" which could result in two events:

   - An increase in secondary mortgage market activity because the points on a loan sold can be taken into immediate income.

   - An increase in options available to borrowers that would include low - or
     no - point loans with correspondingly higher interest rates.

2. List and discuss the advantages and disadvantages of retail versus wholesale mortgage origination.

   ANSWER: The students should list most of the following: wholesale lending is generally a lower cost way of loan origination; allows the lender to move quickly in and out of markets that are hot; allows for servicing to be acquired at a lower cost. On the other hand, retail lending generally allows for higher loan quality; can be profitable with fewer loans per production personnel; may result in higher fee income.

3. The **Mortgage Bankers Association of America** estimates that each residential mortgage loan mortgage bankers originate has a cost of about $1,700 per loan. Why is the cost so high? How can a mortgage lender overcome this initial loss?

   ANSWER: These figures apply specifically to mortgage bankers but are also probably applicable to all mortgage lenders that pay loan originators a commission. Also mortgage bankers originate mostly FHA and VA loans that have either administratively set origination points (VA loans) or points that are kept low by market pressures.

   Lenders who face this situation are able to continue in business because they are often able to make a slight profit on marketing the loans when the loans are sold in the secondary mortgage market. These lenders may also make a profit from the warehousing of the loan(s) before sale. Finally, the most important way of making up for the initial origination loss is from the income generated by the servicing function. Typically, a loan becomes profitable in the third, fourth or fifth year, depending on the extent of the initial loss.

ANSWERS TO ORAL DISCUSSION POINTS

The discussion points at the end of each chapter are intended for oral discussion in class. Suggested answers/points to emphasize to the questions are found below.

1.   Discuss the five keys for a successful lending operation.

> **ANSWER:** For any residential mortgage lender to have a successful first mortgage program five elements must be in place. These five elements are:
> - Loan demand,
> - Product offerings,
> - Trained personnel,
> - Specific marketing and
> - Competitive pricing.

2.   Identify the various methods of loan origination. Discuss the pros and cons of each method.

> **ANSWER:** In today's rapidly evolving primary mortgage market, four strategies or methods of loan origination are used:
> - Retail loan origination (Pro: traditional method still used by most originators, superior customer service. Con: most expensive way to originate)
> - Wholesale loan origination (Pro: lower cost of production, ability to move quickly into and out of markets. Con: fraud?, lower customer service)
> - Combination of retail and wholesale loan origination
> - Internet or online is rapidly becoming a fourth strategy - at the present time only a small percentage of mortgage loans are originated using this strategy.

3.   What functions are normally performed by a retail loan originator?

> **ANSWER:** The retail mortgage lender directly performs the following origination functions:
> - Completes application with borrower,
> - Verifies all employment, income, and deposits,
> - Orders appraisal,
> - Obtains a credit report,
> - Prepares loan for underwriting/automated underwriting
> - Underwrites the loan application,

- Approves or rejects the loan application,
- Closes and funds approved loan,
- Portfolios or warehouses/sells loan.

4. What features or attributes attract consumers to a particular mortgage lender?

ANSWER: The three "attributes" considered the most important by mortgage lenders in this survey in attracting consumers who are new to an area were: (1.) Referral by real estate sales agents, (2.) Low interest rates on loans, (3.) Good company reputation.

The next four were of about equal importance: (4.) Friendliness of loan officers, (5.) Previous experience with company/institution, (6.) Recognition of company/institution name, (7.) Availability of various loan products, and (8.) Convenience of home or office application.

5. Many mortgage lenders compensate their originators by commission – what is the typical commission for a loan officer – how is it calculated?

ANSWER: The commission normally given to a retail mortgage loan originator is 1/2 of 1 percent of the loan amount (or, as normally stated, 50 basis points). This commission is payable of course, only if the loan can be made according to the policies and procedures of the lender and finally, closes. Some lenders will give a smaller commission per loan until a certain quota has been reached, and then increase the commission to a higher amount, say 60 basis points.

6. How do mortgage originators offset their expenses in producing a residential mortgage loan? What are the expenses in originating a residential loan?

ANSWER: Most retail mortgage lenders charge an application fee or origination points or both to offset some or all of the expenses incurred in performing the various origination functions. If the borrower is charging an application fee, that fee is usually large enough to pay for the credit report, appraisal, and any other direct out-of-pocket expense a lender has in processing the loan application. The use of application fees has given way to charging origination points at most lenders, but some charge both. Origination points are often used by lenders for revenue to accomplish the following: off-set personnel and office expenses,
ncrease yield on mortgages to secondary market requirements, produce current income.
Estimates for the cost of processing a residential mortgage loan (not including the 50 basis points paid to a loan originator) range from 60 to 120 basis points.

CHAPTER 5

MORTGAGE INSTRUMENTS

OVERVIEW OF CHAPTER

This chapter will assist the student in understanding the nature of fixed-rate and adjustable rate mortgages. Within this chapter the student will be exposed to a discussion of why and how the standard fixed-rate, self-amortizing, long-term mortgage was developed in the 1930s. This mortgage has served as a valuable vehicle over the years for putting many millions of American families into a home of their own.

As successful as this mortgage has been, it does not always serve the needs of borrowers and lenders today. One example of this problem is the events of the early 1980s when high inflation and extensive fixed-rate portfolios almost completely bankrupt the thrift industry. One of the answers to this plight of the thrifts and other lenders was the development of alternative mortgage instruments - in particular - the adjustable-rate mortgage (ARM).

Within this chapter, the student will examine the various types of alternative mortgage instruments and how one type may be more beneficial than another.

OBJECTIVES OF CHAPTER

Upon successful completion of this chapter, the students should be able to:

- Discuss how the standard fixed-rate mortgage developed and why it was an important tool for reviving real estate and mortgage lending after the Great Depression.
- Understand that a self-amortizing (direct reduction) mortgage can save the mortgagor a meaningful amount of interest over a term loan.
- Explain the dilemma mortgage lenders were in during the high interest period of the early 1980s and what the consequences of that dilemma were to profitability.
- Describe the components of an adjustable-rate mortgage (ARM).
- Understand the various types of alternative mortgages and

which is more beneficial to the borrower and lender at various times in the interest rate cycle.

- Discuss how the typical adjustable-rate mortgage is priced and how that interest rate can change.

SPECIAL NOTES for class discussion:

The Instructor should make sure students understand that in most local markets the one- year ARMs are offered at a discount from what the index and margin say the rate should be offered. These mortgages are called discounted ARMS (as contrasted with *teaser* rates, which are 300 basis points or more discounted). The reason discounted ARMs are offered should be explained by the fact that many lenders want to restructure their asset/liability mix by placing more ARMs in their portfolio. Thus, they are willing to discount the ARMs to encourage borrowers to select them. Many lenders also offer discounted ARMs because the lender can qualify more borrowers since the borrowers were being qualified at the discounted rate. They are no longer able to do this since both FNMA and FHLMC now require that if an ARM uses the one-year index and is capped at 2 percent then the borrower must be qualified at the maximum rate for the second year.

Another index that may warrant discussion in class is the LIBOR Index (for London Inter-Bank Offering Rate), which has attracted some attention, as American mortgage-backed securities have become more popular in Europe and elsewhere. These foreign investors are more familiar with LIBOR then other indices and if this index is used the mortgages they are used on will be more attractive.

OUTLINE OF CHAPTER

I.   Standard Fixed-Rate Mortgage

      A.   Developed during the 1930s

            1.   Replaced short term loans

            2.   Helped restart mortgage lending

      B.   Direct reduction mortgage

            1.   Self-amortizing

            2.   Save considerable interest over term loan

II.   Mortgage Lenders' Dilemma

      A.   Extensive fixed-rate portfolio

B.   High inflation

C.   Negative spread of over 100 basis points

D.   Sharing the Risk

III.   Adjustable Rate Mortgage

A.   Use of an index

B.   Caps on periodic and lifetime increases

C.   Use of the margin

D.   Qualifying the ARM Borrower

IV.   Types of Alternative Mortgages

A.   Graduated Payment Mortgage

B.   Flexible Loan Insurance Program

C.   Reverse Annuity Mortgage

D.   Shared Appreciation Mortgage

E.   Price Level Adjusted Mortgage

F.   Convertible Mortgage

G.   Reduction Option Loan

H.   Bi-Weekly Mortgage

SUGGESTED TRUE/FALSE QUIZ

1.   Fixed-rate mortgage loans are the norm around the world. **F**

2.   Self-amortizing loans started in England about 400 years ago. **F**

3.   Over the past thirty years variable-rate loans originations have been as high as 60 percent. **T**

4.   Direct reduction mortgage costs more in interest than a year-end payment loan. **F**

5.   The most popular index for an ARM loan is the one-year treasury adjusted to a constant maturity. **T**

6.   The most common margin for an ARM loan is 325 basis points. **F**

7.   A problem with most ARM loans is there is no limit on how much the interest rate may increase. **F**

8.   Discount ARM loan are illegal under most state laws. **F**

9.   A biweekly mortgage requires 24 payments are year. **F**

10.   Reverse Annuity Mortgages are only for people over 62. **T**

MULTIPLE CHOICE QUESTIONS. More than one answer may be correct – select all correct answers. (Correct answers are italicized.)

1.   The maximum interest rate a mortgage lender may charge for an ARM loan is called
   a.   margin
   b.   ***cap***
   c.   discount
   d.   initial adjustment

2.   The primary reason mortgage lenders are interested in ARM loans is to
   a.   limit mortgage choices for borrowers
   b.   ***share interest rate risk with the borrower***
   c.   steady cash flow over the term of the loan
   d.   want to end fixed-rate loans

3.   Reverse Annuity Mortgages are designed for which borrower
   a.   first-time homebuyers
   b.   ***older homeowners***
   c.   borrowers who will be in home for short time
   d.   anyone

4.   The biweekly mortgage loan requires how many payments in a normal year?
   a.   12
   b.   24
   c.   ***26***
   d.   48

5. The 15-year loan is designed for the borrower who wants to
   a. ***save interest when compared to a 30-year loan***
   b. make additional principal payments each month
   c. wants a reduced monthly payment
   d. will only be in home for five years.

SUGGESTED SHORT ESSAY QUESTIONS

1. List and briefly describe the features of at least four alternative mortgage instruments.

   ANSWER:
   Adjustable Rate Mortgage: Index + margin = initial interest rate. Margin is normally 275 basis points. Usually have 2 percent annual cap and 6 percent caps.

   Graduated Payment Mortgage: designed to provide borrowers with an opportunity to match their expected increasing income with a mortgage payment that is initially low but increases yearly. May contain negative amortization.

   Reverse Annuity Mortgage: designed to enable older retired homeowners to use the equity in their homes as supplemental monthly income while still retaining their ownership.

   Shared Appreciation Mortgage: designed to give a borrower a below— market rate in exchange for giving a lender a percentage of any appreciation in value of the home securing the loan.

   Price Level Adjusted Mortgage: designed to keep the <u>real</u> mortgage payment constant over the life of the mortgage. That means, in essence, that the payment increases in step with inflationary increases.

   Biweekly: designed to allow a borrower to match paydays with mortgage payments. This mortgage also saves considerable amount of interest because principal payments are made 26 times a year rather than 12.

ANSWERS TO ORAL DISCUSSION POINTS

The discussion points at the end of each chapter are intended for oral discussion in class. Suggested answers/points to emphasize for the questions are found below.

1. Discuss how the standard fixed-rate mortgage developed in the United States and why it was an important tool for reviving real estate and mortgage lending after the Great Depression.

    ANSWER: Before the Great Depression, most mortgages were short-term; interest only paid every six or twelve months. Because these mortgages needed to be refinanced at the end of the term, many homeowners lost their homes when they could not get refinancing from the financial institutions because of the liquidity crises. The Home Owners Loan Corporation was formed to purchase these mortgages from financial institutions. HOLC would then recast the mortgage as a 20-year self-amortizing mortgage that called for monthly payments of principal and interest. This began the popular use of the 20-year self-amortizing mortgages, and practically all financial institutions began to offer them.

2. Explain why a self-amortizing (direct reduction) mortgage can save a mortgage borrower a substantial amount of interest over a term loan.

    ANSWER: The standard fixed-rate mortgage is a monthly amortized, direct reduction instrument. This means that equal monthly payments for the term of the loan are used to directly reduce the amount owed by first paying interest on the loan due since the last payment and then using the remainder to reduce principal. The direct reduction of principal allows for a considerable savings in the total amount of interest a borrower would have to pay over the life of the loan if interest were calculated on the entire amount of principal, as occurs with a term loan. Term loans allow for no principal repayment during the term - only periodic interest payments, with the entire principal due at the end of the term.

3. Explain the primary reason that adjustable-rate mortgages are used throughout the world with the exception being the United States.

    ANSWER: The primary reason is that every other country has had multiple bouts of inflation that destroys the value of the money to be repaid in the future on a mortgage loan. Only by indexing the payment would lenders be interested in long term mortgage lending.

4. Identify and discuss the components of an adjustable-rate mortgage.

    ANSWER: The student should explain that one of the various Indexes is used which establishes an index rate to which is added the margin (typically 275 basis points). The combination of these two creates the initial interest rate. Practically all ARMS today also contain caps on the periodic and lifetime interest rate increases - usually 2 and 6 percent.

5. What must a mortgage lender do to attract consumers to an adjustable-rate mortgage when fixed-rate mortgages are attractively priced?

ANSWER: In order to make an ARM loan attractive to more consumers, most lenders lower the initial interest rate (and thus the payment rate) from that called for by adding together the index and the margin. This initial rate is called a "discounted" rate and may be 200 basis points or more below the full indexed rate. If the rate is 300 basis points or more, the rate is called a "teaser" rate. Mortgage borrowers should be wary of teaser rates since they often require large loan fees or have larger than normal margins.

CHAPTER 6

RESIDENTIAL MORTGAGE LOAN

ORIGINATION AND PROCESSING

OVERVIEW OF CHAPTER

This chapter begins a more in depth analysis of residential mortgage lending. Residential mortgage loan processing is one of the most important functions in the entire residential loan process. This function is one that the most profitable mortgage lenders do well. Students should understand both the extent of this function and its importance to the smooth operation of any mortgage lender.

In particular, the student should pay attention to the consumer protection laws and understand their requirements. The various verification documents are examined in this chapter along with the credit report.

SPECIAL NOTES for classroom discussion:

An interesting discussion to have with students on the issue of discrimination is to ask them "can mortgage lenders discriminate against anyone?" Probably they will answer "NO", but the correct response should be that lenders can and do discriminate. The most obvious is they discriminate against those without sufficient income and that, of course, is legal. ECOA only says that lenders cannot discriminate "on a prohibited basis."

OBJECTIVES OF CHAPTER

Upon successful completion of this chapter, students should be able to:

- Discuss the importance of the initial interview.
- Describe the type of information provided on an application.
- Explain the major provisions of ECOA, TIL and RESPA.

- Understand the function and components of a credit report and distinguish it from a credit score.
- Describe what constitutes acceptable alternative documentation.
- Explain the information that should be supplied to the underwriter.

OUTLINE OF CHAPTER

I.   Residential loan origination and processing

II.   Initial interview

III.   Application

    A.   Uniform application form

    B.   Information provided

        1.   borrower and co—borrower

        2.   name, address

        3.   income and place of employment

        4.   assets and debts

    C.   Mailing out application forms

    D.   Internet applications

IV.   Qualifying an Applicant

    A.   Debt/Income ratios

    B.   Income

    C.   Self-employment

    D.   Use of tax returns,

    E   Other income

    F.   Assets

V.   Credit History

    A.   Purpose of credit report

    B.   Residential Mortgage Credit Report

    C.   Explanation of code

D.   Credit Scores

E.   Derogatory items

VI.   Collateral

VII. Final Check

SUGGESTED TRUE/FALSE QUIZ (Correct answer is at end of question.)

1. Loan processing today averages about 45 days from start to finish. **F**

2. A mortgage lender should never discourage a person from submitting an application for a mortgage loan. **T**

4. A prequalification involves running the numbers but not giving an opinion on credit approval or denial. **T**

5. Whenever a lender denies credit it must provide the applicant with an adverse action notice. **T**

6. About 25 percent of all residential mortgage applications are received via the Internet. **F**

7. Unemployment benefits or welfare can never be used to qualify for a mortgage loan. **F**

8. If a person is self-employed the risk to the mortgage lender is less than a person with wage or salary income. **F**

9. Credit scores are used on only a third of all mortgage applications. **F**

10. Child support can be used to qualify for a mortgage loan if it can be verified. **T**

MULTIPLE CHOICE QUESTIONS. More than one answer may be correct – select all correct answers. (Correct answers are italicized.)

1. The initial interview for a residential mortgage loan can have four outcomes including:
   a. *Credit decision*
   b. *Formal application*
   c. Processing
   d. Underwriting

2. Which of the following is NOT an acceptable way to submit an application for a first mortgage loan?
   a. By Internet
   b. By mail
   c. In person
   d. *Orally*

3. The secondary mortgage market guideline for total debt to income ratio is:
   a. 30/33 percent
   b. *36/38 percent*
   c. 40/45 percent
   d. 50 percent

4. Acceptable income for qualifying for a residential mortgage loan DOES NOT include:
   a. Wages/salary
   b. Rental income
   c. *Unverified tips*
   d. Annual lottery payout

5. The secondary mortgage market guideline for the amount of gross monthly income that should be spent on housing expenses is:
   a. 20 percent
   b. 25 percent
   c. *28 percent*
   d. 35 percent

SUGGESTED SHORT ESSAY QUESTIONS

1. A woman approaches a bank official at a cocktail party and asked whether she

would qualify for a mortgage loan with her income. The bank official says the secondary mortgage market has guidelines for total debt to gross monthly income and recited those ratios. Discuss whether the bank official acted correctly.

ANSWER: The bank official acted properly. He did not give an opinion, instead he stated facts. If he had asked how much she earned and said that is not sufficient to qualify for a loan – gave an opinion – he is still okay. BUT that statement that she would not qualify would constitute a credit decision and that decision requires a notice of adverse action be provided.

2. Why has Alternative Documentation ("alt doc") become so common in residential mortgage lending?

ANSWER: Many mortgage lenders do not require all of the documentation that used to be required. The primary reason for this is to expedite the mortgage lending process. Rather than use Verification of Employment, lenders will accept payroll stubs and rather than use Verification of Deposit, the lender will accept passbooks. "Alt doc" are usually used when a person has a high FICO credit score.

3. If an applicant is using self-employment income to qualify for a residential mortgage loan, what must the mortgage lender do? Why is this important?

ANSWER: Self-employed borrowers represent the high-risk category for default. Therefore it is critical that a mortgage lender underwrite the application carefully. The lender must rely on the past two-year's federal tax returns to determine the average income for those two years.

4. How should a mortgage lender handle the situation where a mother gives her daughter money for a downpayment on a condo?

ANSWER: The mortgage lender must require the mother to sign a "gift letter" that stipulates the money is a gift and does not have to be paid back. The lender must verify that these funds exist and where they came from.

5. Today many mortgage lenders rely heavily on an applicant's credit score. What is a credit score and why is it important?

ANSWER: Most credit reports today contain a credit score – a numeric rating of the applicant's overall credit history. The credit score is determined by a person's payment history of past debt, how much they owe, the types of credit, and whether they are taking on more debt.

ANSWERS TO ORAL DISCUSSION POINTS

The discussion points at the end of each chapter are intended for oral discussion in class. Suggested answers to the questions are found below.

1.   In what three general ways have mortgage origination and processing changed in the last twenty years?

        ANSWER: First, the length of the processing function has shortened dramatically from 30 – 45 days to normally about a week today. (This has not been true during 2002-03 because of unusually high volume.) Second, lenders no longer use one processing model instead many are used depending upon a person's credit score, loan-to-value, etc. Finally, the order taker of prior years is no more – people have multiple skills today that allows for them to perform multiple tasks.

2.   How has technology impacted mortgage origination and processing (benefits and drawbacks)?
        ANSWER: These recent marketplace changes are a result of improvements in technology in practically all aspects of loan origination and processing, affecting all lenders from the largest to the smallest. The impact of technology on the mortgage industry cannot be overstated – it has allowed for cheaper, quicker mortgage lending. Because the mortgage lending industry relies so heavily on data management and cost efficiencies, significant improvements in technology have far-reaching effects and transform the way in which the industry operates. Computer software programs designed for mortgage origination enable processors to accomplish work faster and manage more loans efficiently. These software programs greatly increase the capacity of a single processor. They allow processors to handle more functions, perform many calculations, accommodate more loan programs, save computer keystrokes, produce reports, and operate more reliably than when vendors first introduced them.

3.   What documentation should a consumer bring to a mortgage lender when applying for a loan?

        ANSWER: Names in which title will be held and how title will be held (e.g., joint tenants), address of property to be financed and, if available, its legal description, birth date and social security number for use by credit bureau, principal residence address history for previous two years. Financial Information (for **_all_** applicants) income history for the prior two years, additional or supplemental income history (verified same as above), if self-employed, the most recent two years signed, complete federal income tax returns and an accountant-prepared balance sheet and income statement for the current year, creditor and account number information: credit cards, revolving charge, installment or automobile loans, current and past mortgages, etc.

4.   What special challenges do Internet applications present?

ANSWER: Today, consumers have another option for submitting applications – over the Internet. Internet applications comprised about 10 percent of all originations in 2002, up from only 2 percent in 1995. A lender's website is available around the nation.

While this method of origination may provide more business for the lender and additional convenience for the applicant, it also raises a number of security and compliance issues for the lender. Lenders must ensure this form of origination is consistent with their lending practices and policies and does not create compliance issues. At present, the Internet application process cannot replicate many aspects of this important and effective personal relationship between the loan officer and consumer.

5.   What three issues must a lender identify when qualifying an applicant and why are they important?

ANSWER: loan transaction and program, debt/income ratios, and credit history. These are important because the show ability to repay the debt and willingness to repay.

6.   Discuss the benefits and risks of using alternative documentation loan programs.

ANSWER: To expedite the process the secondary market now accepts for wage or salary income verification "alternative documentation" ("alt doc"), consisting of paystub(s) covering the most recent month and IRS Form W-2s for the most recent two years. The applicant brings originals to the loan officer, who copies them and certifies their authenticity. (This process of lender certification of alternative documentation is the same for verifying income, assets, debts, employment, or anything else.) For employment, alt doc requires a third step: the processor calls the employer to confirm employment and income.

The risks are fraud and not getting enough information to make an informed decision.

CHAPTER 7

UNDERWRITING

THE RESIDENTIAL MORTGAGE LOAN

OVERVIEW OF CHAPTER

Although there is no set formula for underwriting all residential mortgage loans, there is certain information the lender should obtain before making a decision on an application. This chapter explains the importance of the financial capability, the credit history of the borrower and the appraisal of the real estate securing the mortgage. Acceptable ratios for housing expenses and long-term debt for conventional loans sold on the secondary market and FHA loans are compared as well.

OBJECTIVES OF CHAPTER

Upon successful completion of this chapter, students should be able to:
- State the purpose of underwriting guidelines.
- Explain why the initial interview is so important to the underwriting process,
- Compare the housing expense and long-term debt ratios acceptable for conventional loans to those specified for FHA/VA loans.
- List the types of information analyzed by the underwriter in each of these areas; borrower's financial capability, borrower's credit history, and real estate securing the mortgage.
- Understand the issues behind discrimination in mortgage lending and what the Federal Government has done about this activity.

OUTLINE OF CHAPTER

I. Introduction

    A. Definition of underwriting

B.   Three stages of underwriting

C.   No uniform formulas

II.   Underwriting and the Federal Government

    A.   Government-insured loans

    B.   Conventional differs from government-insured loans

III.   Income Ratios

    A.   Monthly Housing expense

    B.   Front-end ratio

    C.   Back-end ratio

    D.   Qualifying the ARM Borrower

    E.   FHA and VA loans

IV.   Employment

    A.   Verification of Employment

    B.   Limited Documentation Programs

V.   Liabilities and Pledged Assets

    A.   Review of credit history

    B.   Bankruptcy

VI.   Loan Application Register

VII.   Property Guidelines

    A.   Purposes of appraisal

        1.   Adequacy of security

        2.   Loan-to-value ratio

    B.   Information evaluated

        1.   Physical security

        2.   Location

        3.   Local government

VIII.   Underwriting Systems

    A.   Judgmental System

    B.   Credit Scoring

IX   The Underwriting Decision

X.   Quality Control

    A.   Key to profitability

    B.   Effective quality control

SUGGESTED TRUE/FALSE QUIZ

1. Underwriting is the process of analyzing risk. **T**

2. In underwriting residential mortgage loans, the lender should follow a strict formula. **F**

3. Uniform underwriting guidelines exist for all residential mortgage loans. **F**

4. When it is obvious that a potential borrower is not qualified, the lender should decline to take the application. **F**

5. Once an application is submitted to the lender, the lender is subject to disclosure requirements. **T**

6. It would be improper for the lender to counsel an applicant during the initial interview. **F**

7. Lenders should have a written underwriting and loan policy to review with potential borrowers. **T**

8. Long-term debt is defined as monthly obligations extending more than three years into the future. **F**

9. Acceptable ratios for housing expenses and long term debt for conventional and FHA loans are both based on gross monthly income. **T**

10. One way of verifying a self-employed applicant's income is to review federal   income tax returns from previous years. **T**

11. HUD-FHA regulations define housing expenses as principal and interest payments. **F**

12. The appraisal establishes the adequacy of the security as well as the loan-to-value ratio. **T**

13. The appraiser in estimating property value considers building codes and zoning ordinances. **T**

14. To reject an application because of the property's location and neighborhood is discriminatory. **T**

15. Income from a part-time job may not be considered when evaluating the financial capability of the borrower. **F**

16. Use of investigative reports relating to the applicant's character and reputation is permissible. **F**

17. Under the Equal Credit Opportunity Act (ECOA), a lender must certify to consumer reporting agencies the purpose for which the credit information is to be used. **T**

18. ECOA permits asking if applicants are married or unmarried. **T**

19. Lenders have **30** days from the date of application in which to notify the applicant whether the loan request has been approved or rejected. **T**

20. Attitude toward credit needs to be considered only when the applicant's income does not qualify. **F**

MULTIPLE CHOICE QUESTIONS. More than one answer may be correct – select all correct answers. (Correct answers are italicized.)

1. Today most residential mortgage loan underwriting decisions are made by:
   a. *Automated underwriting systems*
   b. Experienced human underwriters
   c. Secondary mortgage market
   d. Loan officers

2.	Where are the underwriting guidelines of the secondary mortgage market delineated?
    a.	Statutes of a particular state
    **b.	*Seller/Servicer Guides***
    c.	Local lender's standards
    d.	Federal law

3.	Mortgage lenders look at the "4 Cs" in evaluating an applicant. Which "C" is NOT a part of these "4 Cs":
    a.	Credit
    **b.	*Career***
    c.	Capacity
    d.	Collateral

4.	According to industry studies, this item is considered the best predictor of delinquency.
    a.	Amount of income
    **b.	*Loan to value***
    c.	Age of borrower
    d.	Location of collateral

5.	Credit scores are very important in residential mortgage lending today. What score is the recommended score for streamline or minimal review?
    a.	400
    b.	500
    c.	660
    **d.	*720***

SUGGESTED SHORT ESSAY QUESTIONS

1.	What information is given to and received from the borrower during the initial interview?

	ANSWER: The lender may counsel the borrower if he or she appears to be over-extended but should <u>not</u> discourage the borrower from applying. Disclosures required by ECOA, TIL and RESPA are made at this time. The lender should request information on the borrower's housing expenses, long-term debt, employment history, assets, credit history, and the real estate that will secure the mortgage.

2.	Explain two ways in which the ratios for housing expenses and long-term debt on a conventional loan differ from that on an FHA loan.

ANSWER: The ratios themselves differ. For a conventional mortgage, housing expenses should not exceed 25-28 percent of income while on an FHA loan, the ratio may be as high as 35 percent. Long-term debt on a conventional mortgage should not exceed 36 - 40 percent of income, while on an FHA mortgage it may be as high as 50 percent. The second difference is in the method of figuring income. For conventional loans, gross monthly income is used. The FHA uses net effective income - gross income minus federal income tax - for housing expenses, and the same figure minus FICA and state and local income tax for long-term debt.

ANSWERS TO ORAL DISCUSSION POINTS

The discussion points at the end of each chapter are intended for oral discussion in class. Suggested answers/points to emphasize for the questions are found below.

1.   Identify the types of risks present in residential mortgage lending and which of these does an underwriter evaluate?

        ANSWER: credit, interest rate, collateral, default, compliance, price and market, liquidity, secondary market, portfolio. The underwriter is concerned with the first four and also whether the loan is saleable.

2.   How do underwriting guidelines mitigate the risks in mortgage lending?
        ANSWER: The underwriting analysis quantifies the risk factors present and measures these against other strengths in the file to determine if the strengths offset the weaknesses. The price of the mortgage – the interest rate and points paid by the borrower to the investor – rises **incrementally** with the number and extent of risk factors present in the loan. Although the price of the mortgage increases, the risk of default – and financial loss to the lender, insurer, guarantor, or investor - rises **exponentially** with each additional high risk factor in the loan. Underwriters use the term "risk stacking" to describe this situation.

3.   What are the pros and cons of Automated Underwriting Systems?

        ANSWER: Pros: AUS provide the potential for enormous cost savings and faster approval and closings. As they develop, the capacities and services of these AUS go way beyond providing a credit decision. Now lenders can manage their mortgage pipelines, sell loans to investors, order credit reports, appraisals, flood and tax determinations, etc. all by using an AUS. **Cons:** It is important to recognize that the accuracy and soundness of AUS "recommendations" depend totally on the knowledge, skill, and ability of the person imputting the information. Lenders retain liability for the accuracy of what is submitted.

4.   How do the Loan-To-Value (LTV) and Combined LTV (CLTV) affect the way the underwriter reviews a mortgage application? Why are these so important?

ANSWER: Industry studies find the LTV is the most significant risk factor affecting loan delinquency, default, and loss. It is arguably the most important underwriting ratio and has the greatest single impact on the other underwriting guidelines for an application. 95 percent and higher LTV loans are especially vulnerable as there is no equity in the property if the loan defaults shortly after closing. On the other hand, a low LTV (under 70 percent) may be an indication of the borrower's ability to handle their finances and accumulate wealth. This would be added strength to the application and may offset a weakness, such as high income/debt ratios or low cash reserves.

5.   What compensating factors might offset a total debt ratio that exceeds a lender's guideline?

ANSWER: Higher ratios above 36 percent may be justified by mitigating factors, such as demonstrated ability of an applicant to allocate a higher percentage of gross income to housing expenses, larger downpayment than normal, demonstrated ability of an applicant to accumulate savings and maintain a good credit rating, large net worth, potential for increased earnings because of education or profession.

6.   What are credit scores? How does the secondary market use credit scores and how are they different from mortgage scores?

ANSWER: A credit score is a numeric rating of an applicants' use of debt and credit repayment history. Although the use of credit scores by consumer lenders was common in the 1980's, its use in mortgage lending was not widespread until the proliferation of automated underwriting systems in the mid-1990s. Scores range from the mid 800s (very good) to below 400 (extremely poor). Secondary market guidelines set minimum credit score levels for different loan programs and tailor the level of underwriting review to these "threshold" levels. A mortgage score looks at the credit score AND the loan-to-value, collateral, mortgage type, debt-to-income, etc. for a more comprehensive evaluation.

7.   In what ways does a "Comprehensive Risk Assessment" differ from other underwriting reviews?

ANSWER: "Comprehensive Risk Assessment" is similar to the risk analysis format described in this chapter, but focuses only on default risk. The assessment guidelines are based on the analysis of millions of Fannie Mae mortgage loans. Fannie Mae recommends a lender complete the following steps in this assessment: evaluate primary risk factors, evaluate each contributory risk factor, use information from both evaluations to make a Comprehensive Risk Assessment of the application. The assessment differentiates between "primary" and "contributory" risk factors. Fannie Mae identifies two primary risk factors that most significantly impact default risk: equity investment (LTV and CLTV) and credit history. The lender must consider the combined impact of these factors on mortgage default and identify it as low, moderate, or high primary risk.

CHAPTER 8

GOVERNMENT INSURANCE

AND GUARANTY PROGRMS

OVERVIEW OF CHAPTER

Mortgage lenders and investors both seek methods of reducing risk, which helps to explain the wide use of mortgage insurance and guarantee today. This chapter describes the circumstances that led to the creation of the first government mortgage insurance - Federal Housing Administration (FHA) insurance and Veterans Administration (VA) guarantee programs. These two programs along with USDA guarantees are summarized and compared to those offered by private mortgage insurance companies (PMI -which are covered in Chapter 9, "**Private Mortgage Insurance**").

The chapter starts with a discussion of early mortgage insurance and explains why these early programs did not survive the Great Depression. Although mortgage insurance and guarantee programs are very popular now that was not always the case. The reasons for this are discussed in the first part of this chapter. Finally, the guidelines for processing and underwriting these loans are examined.

OBJECTIVES OF CHAPTER

Upon successful completion of this chapter, students should be able to:
- State the major functions of Federal Government mortgage insurance and guarantee programs.
- Explain how the FHA mortgage insurance program stimulated lending activity among life insurance and mortgage companies,
- List three reasons why use of FHA insurance declined in the 1970s.
- Compare and contrast the basic provisions of FHA

insurance, VA guarantee, and USDA guarantee programs.

OUTLINE OF CHAPTER

I.   Historical Development

    A.   Functions of mortgage insurance

    B.   Mortgage guaranty companies

    C.   FHA insurance

        1.   Mutual Mortgage insurance Fund

        2.   Opposition to FHA legislation

        3.   Life insurance companies as lenders

        4.   How FHA increased home ownership

    D.   Mortgage-lending benefits derived from FHA

II.   FHA Insurance Today

    A.   Section 203 (b)

    B.   Processing and documentation

    C.   Income and employment

    D.   FHA ratios

    E.   Eligibility

III. Veterans Administration

    A.   History

    B.   Eligibility

    C.   Restoration of Veterans' Entitlement

IV.   U.S. Department of Agriculture

    A.   Rural Housing Services Guarantee

    B.   Single Family-Loan Guarantee Program

SUGGESTED TRUE/FALSE QUIZ

1. Mortgage insurance reduces risk and increases the liquidity of a mortgage investment. **T**

2. Mortgage insurance encourages lenders to make more loans with low downpayments. **T**

3. Mortgage guaranty companies were heavily regulated in the 1920s and 30s. **F**

4. Most mortgage guaranty companies had adequate reserves to withstand the Depression years. **F**

5. Careless underwriting and appraisal procedures contributed to the failure of mortgage guaranty companies in the 1920s. **T**

6. FHA-insured mortgages reduced risk to investors by establishing standards for the borrower and the property. **T**

7. Mortgage companies make FHA-insured loans in areas with capital shortages and sell the loans in capital surplus areas. **T**

8. FHA-insured loans offer an attractive yield to investors because of to the dramatically higher interest rates. **F**

9. The ceilings set for the maximum FHA-insured loan amount often fall behind the cost of real estate. **T**

10. The length of time required to obtain a commitment from FHA contributed to the decline in the program's usage in the 70s. **T**

MULTIPLE CHOICE QUESTIONS. More than one answer may be correct – select all correct answers. (Correct answers are italicized.)

1. Under current provisions the maximum loan amount permitted under FHA program Section 203(b) is:
   a. $150,995
   b. $203,000
   c. *$261,609*
   d. $350,000

2. During the 1970s FHA insurance declined in the number of loans insured. The following are reasons for this decline EXCEPT:
   a. Internal reorganization within HUD
   b. ***Not many loans being originated in national economy***
   c. Fraud, abuse and influence peddling by some lenders
   d. Excessive government red tape.

3. The FHA guidelines for ratios for housing expenses and total debt to gross monthly income are:
   a. 25/30
   b. ***29/41***
   c. 30/45
   d. 45/50

4. Under the VA-guaranteed loan program, the current maximum loan guarantee is:
   a. $20,000
   b. $40,000
   c. ***$60,000***
   d. $80,000

5. The following are eligible for a VA-guaranteed loan EXCEPT:
   a. Qualified current or former armed service personnel
   b. Un-remarried surviving spouses of service-related injury or ailment
   c. ***Firemen and policemen***
   d. National Guard reservists who were on active duty for prescribed period

SUGGESTED SHORT ESSAY QUESTIONS

1. What are the advantages and disadvantages of FHA-insured and VA-guaranteed loans to the lender?

   ANSWER: FHA and VA loans appeal to many lenders because of the high amount of insurance protection offered. They are also saleable in the secondary market. Some disadvantages include the interest rate, which is usually below the market rate, the processing time required, and the extensive government regulations involved in these loans.

2. In what ways is private mortgage insurance preferable to FHA insurance or VA guarantees, from a lenders point of view?

ANSWER: The insurance premium for PMI is lower than that for FHA after the first year, and may be dropped when the loan-to-value ratio reaches 80 percent. The coverage is available to a wider group of borrowers than are VA benefits. Conventional rates are more favorable, and there is no loan limit under the PMI program. Processing time is shorter, and some mortgages covered by PMI may contain due-on-sale and prepayment clauses.

3. Explain what the statement means "FHA is not a lender."

ANSWER: FHA – a division of HUD – does not make mortgage loans; it provides insurance that the loan will be repaid when due and thus protects the mortgage lender of the loan. FHA does approve the appraisal, the property and the qualifications of the borrower but does not advance any money to a borrower.

4. Explain what is the purpose of VA-guaranteed loan.

ANSWER: In recognition of the sacrifices made by members of the military, Congress enacted the *Servicemen's Readjustment Act*, which provided, among other things, for a loan to be guaranteed by the Federal Government. Because of this guarantee, lenders were willing to make loans to qualified veterans and active duty servicemen with no downpayment. Basically, purpose of the program is to reward servicemen for service and recognize that part of the sacrifice was financial.

5. What is the purpose of the USDA's Rural Housing Services Guarantee program?

ANSWER: The purpose was to help borrowers (who meet income qualifications) in rural areas of the country to obtain financing for the purchase or construction of a home. It also provides for the funding for housing rehabilitation and preservation, farm labor housing and community facilities.

ANSWERS TO ORAL DISCUSSION POINTS

The discussion points at the end of each chapter are intended for oral discussion in class. Suggested answers/points to emphasize for the questions are found below.

1. Discuss the positive and negative ways in which government-sponsored mortgage programs impact housing.

ANSWER: The social benefit derived from government-sponsored mortgage insurance/guarantees is that it allows for more people to purchase homes. The reason is that lenders are willing to accept smaller downpayments than the normal 20 percent if one of the types of mortgage insurance/guarantees is present. The negative aspect of government-sponsored mortgage insurance/guarantees is the fraud the occurred as the result of greed, appraisers, mortgage lenders and others.

2. How is mortgage insurance (FHA or PMI) different from a mortgage guarantee (VA or USDA)?
   ANSWER: The major difference is mortgage insurance requires the borrower to pay a premium for the insurance that protects the lender. A guarantee that protects a lender does not require a premium. Both government-sponsored programs are available only to select people.

3. Why has FHA mortgage lending increased so dramatically in recent years?

   ANSWER: The program has attracted many first-time homebuyers because of the low downpayment requirement. Also, nearly 35 percent of all FHA borrowers are minorities. Both groups are rapidly growing demographic groups.

4. Explain how FHA mortgage programs differ from conventional mortgage programs.

   ANSWER: FHA insurance is government sponsored therefore has more red tape and delays. It features a low downpayment – 3 percent – for qualified borrowers. HUD scrutinizes the entire mortgage process. Maximum loan is currently $261,609 for high cost areas. Conventional mortgage programs have no federal involvement – and there is no maximum loan amount. Downpayments are not controlled although private mortgage insurance may be required if the downpayment is under 20 percent.

5. How do VA guarantee programs work?
   ANSWER: The Veterans Administration will guarantee to mortgage lenders the repayment of a loan made to qualified veterans (or others in certain circumstances) who do not have to make a downpayment. The guarantee is up to $60,000, which takes the place of the downpayment.

6. What eligibility issues and restrictions does VA impose?

   ANSWER: VA-guaranteed loans are only available to qualified current or former armed service personnel, un-remarried surviving spouse of a veteran whose death was caused by a service-related injury or ailment, or spouse of member of the armed services who has been either missing in action or a prisoner of war for more than 90 days, active duty personnel and National Guard Reservists.

CHAPTER 9

PRIVATE MORTGAGE INSURANCE

OVERVIEW OF CHAPTER

The successes of the FHA insurance program and the VA guarantee program eventually led to the development of a private mortgage insurance (PMI) program. The importance of PMI
today is that many more Americans are able to purchase a home with as little as 5 percent down (in some cases nothing down!). Further, the existence of PMI allowed for these loans with low downpayments to be sold in the secondary mortgage market. The strengths of the PMI companies are examined as well as some of the problems that have appeared over the past twenty years.

OBJECTIVES OF CHAPTER

Upon successful completion of this chapter, the students should be able to:

- Identify factors contributing to the failure of mortgage guarantee companies in the 1930s.
- Discuss how PMI companies reappeared and why.
- Understand why private mortgage insurance is so important in today's market place.
- Explain how mortgage insurance coverage is established
- Discuss how claims are handled by MI companies.

OUTLINE OF CHAPTER

I. Why is Private Mortgage Insurance so Important in Today's Market?

II. Private Mortgage Insurance – Recent History and Evolution

    A. Reasons for MIC growth

    B. Loan Quality

    C. 1980s: Difficult Years

SUGGESTED TRUE/FALSE QUIZ

1.   The first private mortgage insurance company was formed in 1959. **F**

2.   Over the past five years private mortgage insurance has insured twice the dollar amount of federal insurance/guarantee programs combined. **T**

3.   During the 1980s mortgage insurance companies suffered because of origination and servicing "irregularities". **T**

4.   The secondary mortgage market requires mortgage insurance (or some other credit enhancement) if the LTV is over 80 percent. **T**

5.   States require that mortgage insurance companies have $5 of capital for every $25 of risk they insure. **F**

6.   Pool insurance can be used for a group of mortgages even if the LTV of these mortgages is over 80 percent. **T**

7.   In some situations a mortgage lender may grant a "piggyback" loan that has a combined LTV of 95 percent and require no mortgage insurance. **T**

8.   If a claim is submitted to a mortgage insurance company the MI could pay off the claim and take title to the real estate. **T**

9.   Mortgage insurance is good for the lender because it will last the life of the loan. **F**

10.   If the LTV of a loan is 90 percent, the secondary mortgage market

requires mortgage insurance coverage to 60 percent. **F**

ANSWERS TO ORAL DISCUSSION POINTS.

The discussion points at the end of each chapter are intended for oral discussion in class. Suggested answers/points to emphasize to the questions are found below.

1.   How is private mortgage insurance (PMI) different from government insurance and guarantee programs?

   ANSWER: Basically the federal government is not involved with private mortgage insurance. MI companies offered an alternative to the successful VA and FHA mortgage insurance programs for which many consumers and some properties were ineligible. The return of private mortgage insurance was important for potential homebuyers who had difficulty saving the 20 percent downpayment and did not qualify for either FHA or VA loans. Further, mortgage lenders not offering FHA or VA programs could now approve a mortgage with small downpayments – if the mortgage was covered by private mortgage insurance.

2.   Explain the recent growth of PMI compared to government-sponsored programs?

   ANSWER: Since 1997 PMI companies have insured more than *twice* the dollar amount of mortgage debt in the United States than these federal government insurance programs combined.   In 2001 nearly 64 percent of the dollar volume of **insured** mortgage originations was provided by private mortgage insurance (30 percent FHA, and 6 percent VA). The reason for the strength of the PMI is fewer people qualify for VA loans and FHA loan limits placed restraints on the growth of FHA insurance while MI was available to more people.

3.   What is "pool" insurance and how is it used?

   ANSWER: A recent trend for MI companies has been to insure pools of mortgages. These mortgages are not necessarily over 80 percent LTV, but instead may present some other greater risk than traditional "investment quality" secondary market loans (for example, lower credit scores, no income verification, etc.). The MI company will insure the entire pool of loans to improve them to investment grade. Usually the pool insurance reduces both investor and MI company exposure to a certain percent of the original pool loan amount that is negotiated, usually 5 to 25 percent.

4. How have PMI companies performed in 1980's and 1990's? Why the difference?

    ANSWER: In the 1980s the economic situation changed and the MI industry suffered spectacular losses with $5 billion paid out in claims to policyholders. Dramatic increases in inflation and interest rates resulted in a generally slowing of property appreciation in most areas and significant property depreciation in entire regions of the country. As a result, many homeowners could not sell their property and pay off their mortgages to avoid foreclosure. Also lenders in the '80s had some questionable lending and servicing problems.
    In the 1990s the PMI companies benefited tremendously as a result of the economic expansion throughout the decade, a welcome period after the painful 1980s. Although current business and financial performance for PMI companies was stellar, the PMI companies had learned a painful lesson in the 1980s and in the 1990s developed programs that would hedge the potentially negative effects of a poor home purchase market.

5. Discuss how PMI impacts the housing market and the secondary mortgage market.

    ANSWER: In a nutshell, PMI allows more people to qualify for a mortgage loan with a low downpayment thus stimulating the housing market and, as a result, increasing the sale of mortgages into the secondary mortgage market.

6. How do you calculate a PMI premium?

    ANSWER: First, the amount of coverage must be established. The amount of coverage depends on the LTV. The premium is then calculated (by each insurer) based upon the amount of coverage desired.

CHAPTER 10

SELLING RESIDENTIAL MORTGAGE

LOANS

OVERVIEW OF CHAPTER

If there is one lesson that all mortgage lenders learned well from the events of the early 1980s, it is that all residential mortgage loans originated should be capable of being sold into the secondary mortgage market. This sale could occur immediately after closing – called on a "flow" basis – or after the loan has become "seasoned". This conclusion is true even if a mortgage lender, at the time of origination, believes that the loans will only stay in the lenders' portfolio. If the mortgage markets should turn in such a way that the sale of loans is essential, then the loans are capable of being sold.

The chapter starts out with a discussion of the pros and cons of the various business strategies for selling loans produced by the origination function. Since most loans originated today are sold to another investor, the details of a sale are discussed.

Most lenders who originate loans that are intended for sale into the secondary mortgage market first obtain a commitment from an investor, which obligates that investor to purchase the mortgages from the originator. The student is exposed to the various types of commitments and what constitutes a valid commitment. Finally, the chapter explains yield and how it is calculated for residential mortgage marketing transactions.

OBJECTIVES OF CHAPTER

Upon successful completion of this chapter, the students should be able to:

- Discuss the various marketing alternatives for loan production
- Explain the details required in a mortgage sale

- Calculate the increased yield to the originator from participation sales
- Explain how yield is calculated
- Calculate the weighted average yield and how to discount a mortgage package

OUTLINE OF CHAPTER

I. Selling Mortgage Loans as a Business Strategy

   A. Most originations should be saleable

   B. Nonstandard mortgages

II. Marketing Alternatives

   A. Retaining production in portfolio

   B. Selling production to FNMA/FHLMC

   C. Directly Issuing MBS

   D. Direct sales to permanent investors

   E. Selling production to conduits

III. Selling loan production to investors

   A. Becoming an approved seller/servicer

   B. MERS

IV. Secondary Mortgage Market Commitments

   A. Development of commitments

   B. Firm commitments

   C. Standby commitments

V. Pipeline Management

VI. What is Yield?

   A. Yield Comparisons

   B. Weighted Average Yield

   C. Price for a Package

SUGGESTED TRUE/FALSE QUIZ

1. Sales to the secondary mortgage market have recently been over $3 trillion a year. **F**

2. A conforming loan is one that is at or below the maximum loan amount for sale in the secondary mortgage market. **T**

3. A nonstandard mortgage loan is one that does not conform to the processing/underwriting standards of the secondary market. **T**

4. Ultimately all mortgage loans can be sold to some investor. **T**

5. Interest rate risk is not considered a reason to sell loans in the secondary market. **F**

6. Because Fannie Mae and Freddie Mac were originally started by the federal government, any mortgage lender can sell loans without being approved to do so. **F**

7. Commitments are critical to successful mortgage lending for those lenders that sell mortgages. **T**

8. The price an investor will pay for a mortgage loan (i.e., the yield on the mortgage) determines the value of that loan in the secondary market. **T**

9. One a loan has been sold to an investor the principle and interest payment belong to the seller until the first of the month. **F**

10. Weighted-average yield is a tool for calculating yield of a single mortgage that is two or more years old. **F**

SUGGESTED SHORT ESSAY QUESTIONS

1. List and briefly discuss the marketing alternatives mortgage lenders have for loan production.

    ANSWER: (1) Retaining production in portfolio - this may be the best investment a lender can make, depending on the market. All loans retained in portfolio should be capable of being sold into the secondary market if necessary. (2) Sell production to FNMA/FHLMC - both of these government related agencies are always in the market and allow the originator to sell in order to shift the market risk to another and also to grow servicing. (3) Directly Issue MBS - if a lender is both large enough and sophisticated enough, it may decide to issue MBSs directly. (4) Direct sales to permanent investors. (5) Sell production to conduits.

2.   If the yield required in the secondary mortgage market is 10.12 percent on a lender's package of $10,000,000 originated with a weighted average yield of 9.9 percent, how would this package be priced to deliver the required yield?

       ANSWER: It would have to be discounted.
       $10,000,000 x 10.12 % = $1,012,000
       $10,000,000 x 9.9% = $ 990,000
       $990,000 div. by .9775 = $1,012,787

ANSWERS TO ORAL DISCUSSION POINTS

The discussion points at the end of each chapter are intended for oral discussion in class. Suggested answers/points to emphasize to the questions are found below.

1.   Describe the business strategy of selling mortgage loans. Why is it the most popular residential mortgage loan strategy today?

       ANSWER: Mortgage bankers always had to sell loans, other lenders, including commercial banks and credit unions, became sellers in the 1980s and 1990s as originations exceeded their ability to portfolio loans. Further, most lenders understood that by selling loans they transfer interest rate risk, credit risk, prepayment risk, etc. to the investor.
       Today, the majority of mortgage originators realize that most residential mortgage loans should be saleable (i.e., capable of being sold) in the secondary mortgage market even though the intent at origination is for those loans to be placed in a lender's portfolio.

2.   What alternatives does a mortgage originator have for the residential mortgage loans that have been originated?

ANSWER: In today's sophisticated mortgage market, all classifications of mortgage lenders have the same strategic alternatives for placement of their loan production. These alternatives include:

1.   Retaining some or all loan production in own portfolio,
2.   Selling whole loans or participations to government sponsored enterprises - Fannie Mae/Freddie Mac or Federal Home Loan Banks,
3.   Selling whole loans or participations to private secondary market entities,
4.   Directly issuing mortgage-backed securities (MBS),
5.   Selling loans to conduits for packaging into MBS.

3.   Identify and discuss the inherent risk of residential mortgage origination.

ANSWER: In addition to the economic functions performed by the secondary mortgage market, the secondary market helps mortgage originators manage the following risks:

- Credit risk,
- Interest rate risk,
- Prepayment risk, and
- Liquidity risk.

4.   What are the major benefits that a mortgage lender derives from selling loans into the secondary mortgage market?

ANSWER: The advantage gained from selling loans to these major secondary market players or other participants is based on the following factors:

- No portfolio risk from changing interest rates,
- Increased ability to meet local housing demand,
- Instant liquidity,
- Increased servicing volume and income,
- Potential for marketing profit,
- Participation leverage.

5.   What steps must a mortgage lender go through before it can sell loans into the secondary market?

ANSWER: Before any mortgage lender can sell mortgage loans to any investor it must become an approved lender with that investor. Fannie Mae and Freddie Mac refer to approved lenders as Approved Seller/Servicers. As a general rule, a mortgage lender must be approved to be both a seller of loans and servicer of loans.

6.   What are loan commitments and why are they so important in secondary mortgage market transactions?

ANSWER: Commitments are critical to successful mortgage lending for those lenders that sell mortgages. A commitment is an undertaking by either a mortgage lender to make a loan or an investor to buy a loan. A commitment is legally binding as a contract if it agrees completely with the loan application or the offer to sell. The reason commitments are so important is that interest rates can move quickly and if a lender is not "covered" they could lose a lot of money when loans are actually sold.

7.   Explain the pricing options that a lender has when selling loans into the secondary mortgage market.

ANSWER: The secondary mortgage market players (meaning in this context, Fannie Mae and Freddie Mac) through posted yields, establish the price they will pay for a net yield (or pass-through rate) on a residential mortgage. Investors will buy mortgage loans at: **Par**, (100 percent of face value), **Discount**, (e.g., price of 98 – or 98 percent of the loan amount - for a 9 percent net yield equals 9.184 yield), **Premium,** (e.g., price of 102 – or 102 percent of the loan amount - for a 9 percent net yield equals 8.823 yield).

CHAPTER 11

SECONDARY MORTGAGE MARKET

OVERVIEW OF CHAPTER

This chapter explains the reason why a secondary mortgage market is required and important to residential~ mortgage lending. This chapter also describes the economic functions of the secondary market. However, the greatest portion of the chapter deals with the three organizations active in the secondary market - FNMA, GNMA and FHLMC. Their sources of financing, and methods of buying and selling mortgages are described. The chapter closes with a summary of the uniform documentation developed by FNMA and FHLMC.

Although mortgage-backed securities (MBS) have been a part of mortgage lending since the 1920s, they have only recently achieved the dominant position they hold in residential mortgage lending. Part of this chapter is designed to expose the student to MBS by first explaining the reasons for MBS. From the basic concept of MBS, the student next examines the various types of MBS. Although FHLMC and FNMA have been major players in issuing MBS, GNMA was the first to issue the modern MBS with a guarantee of timely payment of principal and interest. This governmental agency is examined along with the functions it performs.

OBJECTIVES OF CHAPTER

Upon successful completion of this chapter, students should be able to:

- Distinguish between the primary and secondary mortgage market.
- Describe the economic functions of the secondary mortgage market.
- Compare FNMA's, GNMA'S and FHLMC's methods of financing mortgage purchases.
- Summarize the mortgage purchase programs used by each of these secondary market institutions
- Explain the importance of Uniform Documentation to the mortgage market.

OUTLINE OF CHAPTER

I. Introduction

    A. Growth of residential Lending

        1. Availability of mortgage funds at reasonable rates

        2. Currently over 50 percent of originations are funded in the secondary mortgage market

    B. Distinction between primary and secondary mortgage markets

II. Economic Functions of the secondary Market

    A. Provide liquidity

    B. Moderate cyclical flow of mortgage capital

    C. Assist flow of capital from surplus to deficit areas

    D. Lessen geographical spread in interest rates and allow diversification

III. Financial institutions Active in the Secondary Market

    A. FNMA

        1. Historical Development

        2. Financing mortgage purchases

        3. FNMA Earnings

        4. Continuing Problems

        5. Secondary market operations

        6. Types of mortgages purchased

    B. FHLMC

        1. Historical Development

        2. Participation program

        3. Source of financing

        4. Participation Certificates (PCs)

        5. Guaranteed Mortgage Certificates (GMCs)

II. Mortgage Backed Securities (MBSs)

A. Concept

B. Private Secondary Mortgage Market

C. GNMA

SUGGESTED TRUE/FALSE QUIZ

1. Approximately 50-60 percent of each year's originations are purchased by the secondary mortgage market. **T**

2. Both Fannie Mae and Freddie Mac are private corporations. **T**

3. Fannie Mae and Freddie Mac combined own about 50 percent of all outstanding U.S. residential debt. **F**

4. Although both Fannie Mae and Freddie Mac are successful, Fannie Mae averages about 50 percent more loans purchased each year. **T**

5. Ginnie Mae was once a part of Freddie Mac. **F**

6. Fannie Mae purchases all types of single-family mortgages loans but never multi-family. **F**

7. According to the most recent statistics nearly one-third of loans purchased by Fannie Mae had credit enhancements. **T**

8. Freddie Mac was originally formed to serve members of the Federal Reserve System. **F**

9. Recourse can be defined, as the contingent liability a seller of a mortgage loan has to repurchase the loan if the sale breaches on one of the warranties the seller made. **T**

10. A mortgage-backed security is a capital market security. **T**

SUGGESTED QUIZ (Use instead of multiple choice).

<u>Directions</u> Each of the following statements describes some aspect of the Federal National Mortgage Association (FNMA), the Government National Mortgage

Association (GNMA), or the Federal Home Loan Mortgage Corporation (FHLMC). Fill in the initials of the appropriate organization(s) in the space to the right of each statement.

1. It is the largest single owner of residential mortgage debt. <u>FNMA</u>
2. Its entry into the secondary mortgage market led to the development of uniform documents for conventional mortgages. <u>FHLMC</u>
3. It guarantees timely payment of principal and interest on securities backed by FHA/VA loans. <u>GNMA</u>
4. It purchases FHA-insured, VA-guaranteed and conventional mortgages. <u>FNMA</u>
5. It retains many of the mortgages it purchases. <u>FNMA and FHLMC</u>
6. It was originally created for the use of the members of the FHLB System. <u>FHLMC</u>
7. It sells Mortgage Participation Certificates to thrifts and Guaranteed Mortgage Certificates to bank trusts and pension funds. <u>FHLMC</u>
8. It is a federally supervised but privately owned corporation. <u>FNMA and FHLMC</u>
9. It is a part of HUD and is funded through the federal budget. <u>GNMA</u>
10. It finances its operations through the sale of discount notes and debentures. <u>FNMA and FHLMC</u>

SUGGESTED SHORT ESSAY QUESTIONS

1. Explain the difference between the primary and secondary mortgage markets.

    ANSWER: The primary mortgage market consists of lenders originating mortgages and extending the funds directly to the borrower. The secondary mortgage market consists of primary lenders and permanent investors buying and selling mortgages from each other.

2. What are the benefits of uniform documentation to lenders and investors in the secondary mortgage market?

    ANSWER: Lenders that use uniform documents at the time of origination are assured that the documentation of loans will allow the loans to be saleable in the future assuming all other features are acceptable to investors. Investors across the country will be exposed to the same documentation regardless of where the loan was originated can review a package for purchase without being confronted by different forms from each region.

3.	Discuss the basic reason why MBS were reintroduced in the late 1960s. Why were they accepted so well this time by investors?

ANSWER: The basic concept behind MBS was to provide more funds for housing. Traditional lenders no longer had sufficient funds to provide for the housing that was needed by a growing population. Through the use of MBS it was believed that funds from such non-mortgage lenders as pension funds could be used to provide the needed funds for housing, since MBS are capital market securities with the payment of principal and interest guaranteed.

ANSWERS TO ORAL DISCUSSION POINTS

The discussion points at the end of each chapter are intended for oral discussion in class. Suggested answers/points to emphasize for the questions are found below.

1.	What economic functions are performed by the secondary mortgage market?

ANSWER: (1) Provides liquidity. The secondary market is an accessible market for investors who need funds and must liquidate their purchases. (2) Moderates the cyclical flow of mortgage capital. Secondary market organizations like FNMA can purchase existing mortgages when no other investors are able, protecting the market from frequent slumps. (3) Assists flow of capital from surplus to deficit areas. An investor in an area with excess funds can purchase mortgages from a lender in another region that has a demand for funds. (4) Lessens geographical spread in rates and allows diversification. Constant movement of funds from one region to another prevents a capital shortage area's rates from increasing dramatically over another areas rates. Diversification reduces risk.

2.	Identify the major players in the secondary market and their specific roles.

ANSWER: The players are Fannie Mae, Freddie Mac, Federal Home Loan Banks and Ginnie Mae. The first three purchase mortgage loans although Fannie Mae and Freddie Mac are dominant. Ginnie Mae's role is to provide the "full faith and credit of the federal government" to mortgage-backed securities.

3.	What types of mortgage loans will Fannie Mae and Freddie Mac buy?

ANSWER: Basically all types of residential mortgage debt including conventional, FHA/VA single-family loans and also multi-family loans.

4.   What is the difference between "whole loan" sales and "participation sales"?

ANSWER: Whole loan sale is a sale of a 100 percent interest in the loan or pool of mortgages while participation sale is the sale of a portion (e.g. 90 percent) of a loan or pool of mortgages with the remaining amount staying with the originator.

5.   What is "credit enhancements"? Why is it important to today's market?

ANSWER: Both secondary mortgage market investors are required by their charter from the federal government to obtain mortgage insurance on all mortgage loans if the loan-to-value (LTV) ratio at the time of purchase is greater than 80 percent. In the past this meant mortgage insurance or guarantee was required for all loans if the LTV was over 80 percent. Today, both GSE will allow loans with over 80 percent LTV to be purchased without mortgage insurance or guarantee if another form of "credit enhancement" is available. This could take the form of pool insurance on a large group of mortgage loans or recourse arrangements whereby the seller agrees to repurchase loans that become delinquent. Credit enhancements are important in today's market because it allows borrowers to get LTV over 80 percent without having to pay for mortgage insurance.

6.   What does "recourse" mean? How can a lender avoid this risk?

ANSWER: Recourse can be defined, as the contingent liability a seller of a mortgage loan has to repurchase the loan if the sale breaches on one of the warranties the seller made.
A lender can avoid this risk by producing loans according to the investor's guidelines.

7.   What are mortgage-backed securities? Why are they so important?

ANSWER: MBS now constitute the largest classification of holders of residential debt, with over $3 trillion outstanding at the end of 2002 – thus the reason for their importance. MBS are capital market securities that consist of a pool of mortgages often insured or guaranteed.

CHAPTER 12

RESIDENTIAL REAL ESTATE APPRAISAL

OVERVIEW OF CHAPTER

This chapter examines the important function of appraising residential real estate. The appraisal of residential real estate is the process of estimating value with the goal of providing adequate security to a lender. The appraisal process has been controversial at time over the past twenty years because of increased delinquencies in certain parts of the country. This chapter defines value and explains the factors that determine it. The steps in the appraisal process are outlined and three different approaches to value are described: market data, cost and income. Basic formulas for calculating value and applications for each approach are included in this chapter. An explanation of how the three approaches are correlated into a single estimate of value completes the chapter.

OBJECTIVES OF CHAPTER

Upon successful completion of this chapter student should be able to:

- Define residential appraisal
- List six reasons for appraising real estate
- Define market value
- Name the three approaches to value and state how each computes estimated value.
- Distinguish between reproduction cost and replacement cost
- Describe three types of depreciation
- Explain how the gross rent multiplier technique is used to estimate value in residential property
- Compare and contrast the application or uses of the three approaches to value

OUTLINE OF CHAPTER

I.   Introduction

A. Definition of appraisal

B. Purposes of appraisal

II. Uniform Residential Appraisal Report

III. Principles of Real Estate Value

    A. Market value

    B. Market price

    C. Factors changing value

    D. Basic value determinants

        1. Supply and demand

        2. Highest and best use

        3. Diminishing returns

        4. Substitution

IV. The Appraisal Process

    A. Definition of the problem to be solved by appraisal

    B. Market data approach

        1. Comparable properties

        2. Adjustments to value

    C. Cost appreciation

        1. Reproduction cost

        2. Replacement cost

        3. Depreciation

    D. Income approach

        1. Gross rent multiplier

        2. Net operating Income

        3. Capitalization

V. Correlation of Value

SUGGESTED TRUE/FALSE QUIZ

1.   The appraised value of a piece of real estate will be the same regardless of the purpose of the appraisal. **F**

2.   An appraisal is an estimate of value as of a certain date. **T**

3.   Market value is the price for which a piece of real estate actually sells. **F**

4.   The use of a property that produces the greatest net return over a period of time is called the highest and best use. **T**

5.   Real estate is similar to all other marketable commodities because its value is affected by supply and demand. **T**

6.   The principle of substitution says that the value of the subject property should not exceed the value of a similar property. **T**

7.   The cost approach involves adjusting market value of comparables for physical differences between the comparables and the subject property. **F**

8.   The market data approach is used mainly for appraising single-family residential property. **T**

9.   The depreciation in value due to a loss of economic life caused by wear and tear is known as economic obsolescence. **F**

10.   To determine the gross rent multiplier, the appraiser must know the net operating income and operating expenses of the property. **F**

SUGGESTED SHORT ESSAY QUESTIONS

1.   List six reasons for appraising real estate and identify the one of greatest concern to mortgage lenders.

    ANSWER: An appraisal may estimate:
    1)   Assessed value for taxation purposes
    2)   Insurance value
    3)   Market value for sale or exchange purposes
    4)   Market value for mortgage loan purposes
    5)   Compensation in condemnation proceedings
    6)   Rental value
    The market value for mortgage loan purposes is most important to mortgage lenders.

2.   Identify the approach to value summarized in each of the following formulas.
   a)   cost of reproduction or replacement - depreciation + land value value
          of subject property
   b)   value of comparable property ± adjustments value of subject property
   c)   <u>sale price</u>
          gross income = GRM

       <u>ANSWER</u>
   a)   cost approach
   b)   market data approach
   c)   income approach for residential property

3.   Explain why adjustments to the comparables are necessary for an estimate of
       the value of a subject property.

       <u>ANSWER:</u> A number of comparables should be used to accurately reflect
       the market, and it is likely that some physical differences will exist between
       the comparables and the subject property. A dollar value is placed on each
       feature. Using the sales prices of the comparables as their values, the values
       are increased for features found in the subject property only, and decreased
       for features not found in the subject property. This approach, in effect,
       makes the properties equal and enables the appraiser to estimate the value of
       the subject property more accurately.

4.   Explain how the income approach is used for appraising single-family
       residential property.

       <u>ANSWER:</u> In areas having a rental market in single-family homes, the
       gross rent multiplier method may be used. The sale price of a comparable
       property would be divided by the amount of rent it generated to obtain a
       multiplier. This figure would be multiplied by the monthly rental amount
       received on the subject property to determine its market value.

ANSWERS TO ORAL DISCUSSION POINTS

**The discussion points at the end of each chapter are intended for oral discussion
in class. Suggested answers/points to emphasize to the questions are found
below.**

1.   What two main areas of consideration does an appraisal report help a lender evaluate?

How does the appraisal report do this?

ANSWER: The primary purpose of obtaining an appraisal report is to help the lender determine if the collateral is sufficient security for the loan. The secondary purpose of obtaining an appraisal report is to meet the requirements of state and federal laws and regulations and to sell the loan in the secondary mortgage market. Prudent mortgage underwriting requires that the lender somehow consider the collateral pledged as security for the loan requested. This involves two considerations, and the most commonly used appraisal forms can be divided into two sections to address them: What is the condition of the property? What is the value of the property?

2.   Explain the appraisal process an appraiser would follow developing a traditional appraisal report.

ANSWER: The first step in the appraisal process is to plan the appraisal. Since the appraisal is intended to solve a problem – to estimate value of a particular property – it must be clearly stated as to what type of value is being sought. The process required to produce this estimate of value necessitates identification of the following: (a) real estate to be appraised, (b) type of value being sought, (c) effective date of the appraisal, (d) character of the property, (e) property rights, (f) character of the market in which the property is located.

3.   What three approaches to value are used in developing an appraisal? When is each approach most appropriate?

ANSWER: Appraisers use three very specific appraisal techniques when developing a real estate appraisal: the direct sales comparison approach, the cost approach and the income approach. Direct sales approach is normally used for the typical residential property. The cost approach is used for older properties and the income approach is used for rental properties or if the other approaches do not work.

4.   What factors can affect the market value of the subject property?

ANSWER: Population growth or decline; economic developments; financial factors, such as, the rate of inflation, cost of financing, type of financing available; shifts in consumer preference; governmental regulations, such as, zoning, building codes, taxation; shifts in traffic patterns or public transportation; physical forces, water supply, soil contamination, location on an earthquake fault.

5.   Why are sales comparable adjustments necessary to estimate the value of the subject property?

ANSWER: The market prices of the comparables will be adjusted for the physical differences between the comparable and the subject property. Appraisers "adjust" the features of the sales comp to the subject property. If the sales comp has a feature missing in the subject property, the appraiser calculates a negative adjustment to that sales comp equal to the market value of that feature. If the sales comparable lack a feature present in the subject property, the appraiser makes a positive adjustment to that sales comp.

6.   How do other appraisal forms differ from the Uniform Residential Appraisal Report (URAR)? Why are these differences significant?

ANSWER: The first page of the URAR contains extensive descriptive information about the property, its condition, and the neighborhood in which it is located, and the market conditions at the time of the appraisal. The form provides descriptive information in the following major areas: Subject – address, ownership rights, legal description, occupancy,
Neighborhood – market conditions, price ranges, land use, boundaries, Site – dimensions, zoning, off-site improvements, utilities, flood zone, Description of improvements – exterior, foundation, room count, interior, kitchen, amenities. The second page of the URAR appraisal form develops the three approaches to value (described below) and overall estimate of market value for the property.

7.   Discuss the benefits and drawbacks to a lender using streamlined appraisals and automated valuation models (compared to traditional appraisals).

ANSWER: The main benefit is cost and speed in obtaining the AVM – the main drawback is the interior of the property is not seen.

CHAPTER 13

CLOSING THE RESIDENTIAL LOAN

OVERVIEW OF CHAPTER

The purpose of this chapter is to review those documents required for the closing of a typical residential mortgage loan. These required documents are described and the reason for each document is examined. Students should be made aware that the documents discussed in this chapter are those that generally result in a loan closing but that each state differs in regard to the documents required for a loan closing. In the student's particular state more documents made be required, or fewer. The Instructor may want to discuss what these additional requirements are in the state(s) the students are from.

OBJECTIVE OF CHAPTER

- Describe the purpose of loan closing
- Explain the various ways that loan closing can be handled and by whom.
- Identify the documents required for the closing of a typical mortgage loan.
- Understand the reason behind the required document.

OUTLINE OF CHAPTER

I.   Purpose of residential loan closing

    A.   Protecting the rights of the parties

    B.   Process of loan closing

    C.   Steps in closing a residential mortgage loan

    D.   Commitment letter

    E.   Title insurance

II. Documents Required for a Properly Closed First-Mortgage Loan
   A. First-mortgage checklist
   B. Final requirements
   C. Quality control

SUGGESTED TRUE/FALSE QUIZ

1. The closing of a mortgage loan should not be interpreted to mean that the end of the mortgage-lending process has been reached. **T**

2. The purpose of loan closing is to ensure that the loan is closed according to federal laws and not state law. **F**

3. Most mortgage lenders do not use a commitment letter to inform an applicant that their application has been accepted. **F**

4. The most common method of reviewing legal title and providing protection to mortgage lenders is through the purchase of title insurance. **T**

5. It is important that mortgagors understand that they are not protected under the lender's policy against any defects in their title to the real estate. **T**

6. The amount of title insurance should be equal to the estimated value of the real estate. **F**

7. Names of signers must be consistent though all documents and signatures should be the same as name. **T**

8. Signatures do not have to be notarized if the loan is "federally related". **F**

9. HUD-1 (or HUD-1a) is a requirement of RESPA. **T**

10. If the mortgage transaction is a purchase money mortgage IRS requires real estate brokers to file an informational return showing the gross sales proceeds of the transaction. **T**

MULTIPLE CHOICE QUESTIONS. More than one answer may be correct – select all correct answers. (Correct answers are italicized.)

1. Which of the following is **NOT** a recommend agent to handle the closing of a residential mortgage loan?
    a. Outside attorney
    b. Escrow agent
    c. Title insurance company
    d.   Real estate agent

2. Which of the following are considered a part of residential mortgage loan closing?
    a. Taking the application
    b.   Recording the mortgage
    c.   Disbursement of funds
    d. Underwriting

SUGGESTED SHORT ESSAY QUESTIONS.

1. The term "loan closing" as used in residential mortgage lending refers to the process of completing what steps?

    ANSWER: Loan closing includes the following steps:
    - Formulating, executing, and delivering all documents required to create an obligation to repay a debt and to create a valid security instrument
    - Disbursing the mortgage funds
    - Protecting the security interest of the lender by recording the mortgage
    - Establishing the rights and responsibilities of the mortgagor.

2. The use of a commitment letter is recommended for mortgage lenders – explain the reason for this recommendation.

    ANSWER: The commitment letter serves as the lender's acceptance of the mortgagor's application as submitted. The commitment letter is what creates the contractual right of the borrower to receive a mortgage loan.   It also clearly establishes for the borrower what is expected of them in regard to what has to be done, such as addressing conditions, etc. for the loan to close.

3. What should be contained in a commitment letter?

    ANSWER: The contents of a commitment letter should cover the following

subjects:
- For whom the loan is approved
- The real estate that will secure the loan
- The way the title will be held
- Type of loan (fixed-rate or variable-rate)
- Loan amount
- Interest rate.

4. The secondary mortgage market is very interested in combating mortgage fraud - to that end that they have certain requirements in regards to documentation – list at least five of these requirements?

ANSWER:
- All blanks on Uniform Documents must be completed,
- All corrections on forms must be initialed by the borrowers,
- No liquid paper or correction fluid can be used on the documents,
- Documents should contain original signatures,
- Names of signers must be consistent throughout all documents and signatures should be the same as name,
- Legal description and property address should be consistent throughout and agree with title policy,
- Note and security instrument should be signed on same date,
- Signatures should be notarized according to state requirements.

ANSWERS TO ORAL DISCUSSION POINTS.

The discussion points at the end of each chapter are intended for oral discussion in class. Suggested answers/points to emphasize for the questions are found below.

1. Identify the reasons why residential loan closings are so important to the parties involved.

    ANSWER: A residential mortgage transaction is closed by the delivery of the mortgage (or deed of trust) and note to the mortgage lender and the disbursement of the mortgage funds to the mortgagor or pursuant to the mortgagor's direction. The term loan closing as used in residential mortgage lending refers to the process of: (a) formulating, executing, and delivering all documents required to create an obligation to repay a debt and to create a valid security instrument; (b) disbursing the mortgage funds, and (c) protecting the security interest of the lender or investor (e.g., recording), (d) establishing the rights and responsibilities of the mortgagor.

2.   What are the steps in closing a residential mortgage loan? Who normally handles the closing?

     ANSWER: These steps include the following: (a) advise applicant of loan acceptance by a commitment letter (and, if applicable, set rate, terms, etc.), (b) order final title report (and survey if separate) and any other documents   or verifications still outstanding, (c) schedule closing and prepare closing documents, (d) conduct closing, obtain all required signatures, and disburse funds, (e) return all closing documents to mortgage lender for inclusion in loan file, (f) record mortgage. Loan closing, depending on the law or custom in the jurisdiction, can be handled by any of the following: (a) outside attorney for either the seller or buyer, (b) escrow agent, (c) title insurance company, (d) staff of the mortgage lender.

3.   Why is a commitment letter so important to proper mortgage lending?

     ANSWER: The commitment letter serves as the lender's acceptance of the mortgagor's application as submitted. If the lender makes a counter-offer than the applicant must accept that offer. The commitment letter is what creates the contractual right of the borrower to receive a mortgage loan. It also helps to clearly establish in the borrower's mind what is expected of them in regard to what has to be done, such as addressing conditions, for the loan to close.

4.   What is the purpose of title insurance? Who is protected by title insurance?

     ANSWER: A mortgage lender must establish with certainty that the mortgagor has good title to the real estate that will secure the mortgage debt. The obvious reason is if another person has a superior interest in the real estate securing the mortgage loan and exercises that interest, the mortgage lender will have an unsecured personal loan. A mortgage lender will therefore demand that all questions pertaining to ownership rights be resolved before the loan is closed. The mortgage lender is protected by the title insurance policy paid for by the borrower. If the borrower also wants protection another policy and premium is required.

5.   Why does the Internal Revenue Service need to be informed about a loan closing?

     ANSWER: Agents that close a residential purchase money mortgage are required to report (IRS form 1099-B) the gross sales proceeds to the IRS. If a seller does not cooperate with this report, such as not providing social security numbers, the closing agent could withhold 20 percent of the money due the seller. The purpose is to make sure the IRS knows of capital gains.

CHAPTER 14

MORTGAGE LOAN SERVICING

AND ADMINISTRATION

OVERVIEW OF CHAPTER

One of the most important functions performed by a mortgage lender is that of loan servicing or as it more often called today, mortgage loan administration. This chapter discusses the responsibilities of the servicer and how a loan administration department is typically organized. An explanation of servicing income and the value of a servicing portfolio completes the chapter.

OBJECTIVES OF CHAPTER

- Explain why loan administration is so important to residential mortgage lenders
- Describe the responsibilities of a loan servicer
- List the various functions performed by a loan administration department.
- Explain how the typical functions of loan administration are performed
- Discuss the various ways that a department could be organized
- Explain how servicing income is generated
- Understand why a servicing portfolio has value

OUTLINE OF CHAPTER

I. Purpose of Loan Administration

    A. Loan Administration Defined

    B. Required of all Mortgage Lenders

II. Organization of a Loan Administration Department

III. Servicing Responsibilities and Functions

IV.   Managing Delinquencies and Foreclosures

V.   Portfolio Management and Loan Administration

VI.   Servicing Income

  A.   Other income

  B.   Escrows

VII   Alternatives to Servicing Residential Mortgage Loans

SUGGESTED TRUE/FALSE QUIZ

1.   All residential mortgage loans require servicing. **T**

2.   The originating lender is not required to service a mortgage loan, regardless of whether the particular loan is sold to an investor or held in portfolio. **T**

3.   Servicing responsibilities end when the loan is closed. **F**

4.   Many lenders use the post-closing review as a type of quality control. **T**

5.   A servicing contract establishes the servicing relationship when a mortgage is sold to an investor and the loan originator retains the servicing. **T**

6.   Default on a mortgage loan can only occur if the monthly payment is missed. **F**

7.   The law requires a mortgage lender wait 30 days after a payment was due before beginning collection procedures. **F**

8.   A servicing release premium is paid to an acquiring investor to service loans sold. **F**

9.   All residential mortgage loans require the monthly collection of principle, interest and taxes. **F**

10.   Subservicing describes servicing done by a different department within a lending institution. **F**

SUGGESTED SHORT ESSAY QUESTIONS

1. The activities in mortgage loan administration accomplish three things. Name them and explain how they are carried out.

   ANSWER: Mortgage loan administration performs the required service to the mortgagor, protects the security of the mortgagee, and produces a profit for the servicer. The servicer carries out these objectives by collecting monthly payments and disbursing the investor's share according to the servicing contract, collecting and paying real estate taxes and insurance to protect the investor's interests, and retaining a servicing fee to generate income for the servicer.

2. How are servicing fees computed? By what other means may a servicer earn income?

   ANSWER: The servicing contract specifies the percentage to be retained by the servicer. It is usually a fraction of one percent of the outstanding monthly principal balance, applied only to the payments collected. Servicing income also comes from late payment penalties and transfer or assumption fees.

3. Assume a new residential mortgage lender does not have a sufficiently large servicing portfolio in order to perform the servicing function profitably, what would you advise that company?

   ANSWER: Since the cost of loan servicing is directly tied to the volume of loans serviced, a lender often begins the servicing function with the cost of servicing exceeding the revenue generated by servicing. One way of getting around this problem is to enter into a subservicing arrangement whereby another larger servicer does the servicing for a fee. This subservicing fee is generally lower than the servicing income collected by the originator from an investor therefore allowing the originator to make a profit from servicing.

ANSWERS TO ORAL DISCUSSION POINTS

The discussion points at the end of each chapter are intended for oral discussion in class. Suggested answers/points to emphasize for the questions are found below.

1. Discuss the difference between mortgage loan servicing and mortgage loan administration and how this difference impacts the lender.

   ANSWER: Servicing includes the responsibilities, functions, and day-to-day operations an organization performs over the term or repayment of that loan. Loan administration describes a mortgage servicing department that plays a larger, more sophisticated role in the lender's overall strategy – one that includes servicing loans for secondary market investors. This could be a passive role, where the lender handles only those loans it originates and sells, or it could be a role where the lender actively sells and buys servicing portfolios from mortgage lenders.

2.   Discuss the benefits and drawbacks to a unit vs. functional form of organization for a loan servicing/administration department.

ANSWER: The function system assigns each employee to a specific servicing function, such as real estate taxes, payments, or assumptions. This system allows for specialization, a higher level of service, and if done correctly, speed of operation. The main drawback is that function will not be performed when that person is absent. The unit system assigns small teams of employees to a group of loans where they perform all of the related tasks. All employees can perform each function to cover for each other when absent. The benefit is a more consistent operation. The drawback is no one person is an expert on any one function.

3.   Discuss the various mortgage servicing strategies implemented by lenders.

ANSWER: Several options exist. A lender that sells a loan to an investor may also sell the servicing of that loan to another entity. Some originators (usually mortgage bankers and brokers) sell the loan and servicing before it closes. Others sell it after closing the loan, or sell the loan servicing released, or enter into a sub-servicing arrangement. The point is the valuing and selling of mortgage servicing has grown to where this aspect of mortgage lending is a more significant source of income than the original sale of the loan.

4.   List and explain mortgage servicing functions and responsibilities.

ANSWER: Payment Processing Department has the daily responsibility of applying all payments received and balancing the accounts. **Loan Accounting Department** reconciles loan payments to funds received, notifies investors of distributions of principal and interest less the servicing fee. **Customer Service Department** handles all borrower inquiries and requests, resolves errors and disputes, etc. **Escrow Administration Department** ensures the protection of the security interest by collecting required insurances or credit guarantees. **Collection Department** handles past due loan accounts.

5.   How do refinance waves affect servicing departments (and lenders)?

ANSWER: A "refinance wave" is when a record number of borrowers refinanced at the same time. The effect was devastating to many servicers who see their portfolios evaporate in just a few months. So many borrowers refinanced during these waves that lenders are unable to service the old loans long enough to make a profit on servicing.   Regrettably from the servicers' viewpoint, many mortgagors refinanced their mortgage with another lender, thus the servicing was lost to the other lender.

6.   How would a lender determine its cost of servicing and why is this important?

ANSWER: It is generally assumed that in today's market a mortgage lender must be servicing about $50 million of loans sold to an investor servicing retained before the cost of servicing those loans is offset by the servicing income.   The reason the cost has come down over the years is the increased use of technology and the increase in the average size loan.   The approximately $50 million breakeven point may vary somewhat for different lenders, but as a general rule, appears to be a sound assumption based upon information from the Mortgage Bankers Association of America. As the servicing portfolio of a mortgage lender increases, economies of scale develop. That average annual cost can drop to approximately $100 per loan when the portfolio reaches $1 billion (or about 10,000 loans) and may get as low as $50 when the portfolio reaches $2 or $3 billion.

7.   How are servicing fees calculated? When does a servicer earn these fees?

ANSWER: Servicing fees are earned on loans sold to an investor with the servicing retained. The fee for servicing the sold loans is based upon the unpaid principle balance of the loan. The fee is earned each month when the monthly payment is made by the borrower.

CHAPTER 15

REAL ESTATE LAW and SECURITY

INSTRUMENTS

OVERVIEW OF CHAPTER

This chapter reviews the historical development of real estate law and its importance to all parties involved in real estate and mortgage transactions, the text explains the numerous types of interest in real property, beginning with freehold and leasehold estates. Several types of joint or concurrent ownership are described, as well as methods of transferring land, both voluntary and involuntary. A section on the importance of proper recording completes the chapter.

An understanding of security instruments is a vital part of mortgage lending. This chapter describes the components of a valid mortgage instrument and the similarities and differences between a mortgage and a deed of trust. The rights of both the borrower and lender under various clauses in the mortgage and note are explained. Methods of transferring the mortgaged real estate to another party and procedures for foreclosing defaulted mortgages complete the chapter.

As with prior chapters, the Instructor should advise the students that the real estate law discussed n this chapter is the law as it is generally applied in the majority of states and situations. The laws of an individual state will in all probability differ from the textbook in one or more aspects.

OBJECTIVES OF CHAPTER

Upon successful completion of this chapter, students should be able to:

- Define real property, personal property and fixture.

- Distinguish between freehold and leasehold estates and identify four types of freehold estates.
- Describe three classifications of limited rights to real estate.
- Explain five forms of joint or concurrent ownership.
- Describe eight methods of voluntary and involuntary transfer of land.
- Distinguish between actual notice and constructive notice of recording.
- List the components of a valid mortgage instrument.
- Distinguish between a mortgage and a deed of trust.

OUTLINE OF CHAPTER

I.   Introduction

    A.   Law and real estate inseparable

    B.   Awareness of law necessary for all parties

II.   English Common Law

    A.   Feudal system

    B.   Magna Carta - doctrine of primogeniture

    C.   Alliodial system

III.   Principles of Real Estate Law

    A.   Real property, personal property and fixtures

    B.   Types of estates

        1.   Freehold

        2.   Fee simple absolute

        3.   Defeasible fee simple

        4.   Fee tail

        5.   Life estate

        6.   Leasehold

    C.   Limited rights to real estate

        1.   Easement

        2.   Profit

        3.   Covenant

IV.   Joint or Concurrent Ownership

 A. Joint tenancy

 B. Tenancy by the entirety

 C. Tenants In common

 D. Community Property

 E. Tenancy in partnership

V.   Transfer of Land

 A. Voluntary transfers

  1. Statute of frauds

  2. Quit claim deed

  3. General warranty deed

  4. Special warranty deed

  5. Will

 B. Involuntary transfers

  1. Eminent domain

  2. Adverse possession

  3. Foreclosure and sale

  4. Intestate death

 C. Recording

  1. Actual notice

  2. Constructive notice

  3. Race statute

VI.   Security Instruments

 A. Historical development

 B. American mortgage law

  1. Title theory

  2. Lien theory

 C. The security interest

  1. The mortgage debt

2. The mortgage instrument

3. Clauses to protect the rights of parties

4. Deeds of trust

D. Transfers of mortgaged real estate

1. Free and clear

2. Subject to the mortgage

3. Assumption of the mortgage

4. Assignment of mortgage

VII. Foreclosure and Redemption

A. Default

1. Definition

2. Causes of residential mortgage default

3. Lender's options

B. Foreclosure

1. Judicial proceedings

2. Power of sale

3. Strict foreclosure

4. Entry and possession

5. Deed in lieu of foreclosure

6. Redemption

SUGGESTED TRUE/FALSE QUIZ

1. Real estate law in the U.S. is based upon the Constitution of the U.S. **F**

2. The Feudal System of Land Tenure never had any application in this country. **F**

3. The allodial system recognizes that an owner of real estate has title irrespective of the sovereign and thus owns no duty to the sovereign. **T**

4. When people talk about their ownership of land, they are legally talking about the type of estate they have in real estate. **T**

5. Fee Simple Absolute is the greatest interest a person can have in real estate and it excludes any other interest. **F**

6. A life estate is a freehold estate like the fee simple absolute but it is not inheritable. **T**

7. The most common type of joint ownership of real estate is tenants in common. **F**

8. Community property is the law in all 50 states. **F**

9. An involuntary conveyance occurs when a legal owner of real state loses title contrary to the owner's intention. **T**

10. All state have a "race statute" that dictates that first of two innocent parties to record will be protected. **T**

SUGGESTED SHORT ESSAY QUESTIONS.

1. If A sold land to B but B failed to record and C bought the same land and recorded, what factor determines whether or not C is the rightful owner?

   ANSWER: The protection of C's interest would depend on whether or not there was actual notice. If C knew the land had already been sold, and purchased it anyway, B would be the rightful owner. If C had no knowledge of the prior transaction, purchased the property, and recorded, C's interest would be protected. There are two reasons for this: first, B called to record and give constructive notice, and second, under the "race statute" the first of two innocent parties to record is protected.

2. Explain the difference between the promissory note and the mortgage instrument. What information must be included in a valid mortgage instrument?

   ANSWER: The promissory note is evidence of the borrower's debt. It sets forth the amount due, the interest rate, and payment schedule. The mortgage instrument secures the debt by creating a lien in favor of the mortgagee or by conveying title to a trustee, as in a deed of trust. The mortgage instrument must contain the names of the mortgagor and mortgagee, words of conveyance or a mortgaging clause, description of the debt, description of the real estate, clauses to protect the rights of both parties, the date, signature of the mortgagor, and any other requirement of the state or local government.

3.   If both security agreements are allowed in a jurisdiction, would using a deed of trust, instead of a mortgage, be more advantageous to the mortgagor or mortgagee? Why?

ANSWER: A deed of trust favors the mortgagee. Since title to the real estate has already been conveyed to a trustee, the lender can obtain it more quickly in the event of a default. Also, most states using the deed of trust permit public sale after default without time-consuming court proceedings, and do not grant the mortgagor a statutory right of redemption. The only advantage of the deed of trust to the mortgagor is that no deficiency judgment can be entered against him.

4.   Why would a mortgagor choose to deed the real estate to the lender in lieu of foreclosure? What factors must a mortgagee weigh before accepting the deed?

ANSWER: The mortgagor would not be subject to the embarrassment of a foreclosure suit or be liable for a deficiency judgment. The mortgagee would acquire title immediately and could offer it for sale with no worry of it being redeemed later, since the mortgagor gives up that right. However, the lender must consider the claims of junior lienholders, whose rights are not extinguished by a deed in lieu of foreclosure.

ANSWERS TO ORAL DISCUSSION POINTS

The discussion points at the end of each chapter are intended for oral discussion in class. Suggested answers/points to emphasize for the questions are found below.

1.   What is the term that is used in law to describe, "the greatest interest a person can have in real estate"? Why is this interest not an absolute interest?

ANSWER: Every type of ownership has restraints or limitations on it. It may be subject to easements, eminent domain, or adverse possession. The owner of a piece of land is legally only the owner of an interest in the land. Even a person whose interest is fee simple absolute and who holds all possible rights to the real property is subject to the restrictions described.

2.   What is a "conditional fee"? Give an example of how this transaction could occur.

ANSWER: A freehold estate, which is similar to a fee simple absolute but minus a "stick" (or a right) from the bundle of rights, is a conditional fee simple. This is a freehold estate that could but will not necessarily last forever. An example of a conditional fee simple occurs when conditions are placed on how the property may be used. Grantors of land may put any restrictions they desire on how the land is to be used after it has been conveyed. Grantors can always give less than the full interest they own in conveying land, but never more. They can give possession for any desired period of time, or for any specific use - only as a church, for example.

3.   What is a "legal life estate"? Do they exist today?

ANSWER: A life estate is a freehold estate like the fee simple absolute and others already mentioned, but it is not inheritable. Life estates can be either conventional (created by the grantor) or legal (created by operation of law). The creation of a life estate is a tool often used in estate planning and is a fairly common interest in real estate. By the creation of a life estate the life tenant (the one granted the right) has the use of real estate for a period of time measured by a human life. This estate is common today especially for estate planning purposes.

4.   What is the most common form of joint ownership today in the United States?

ANSWER: Ownership in land can be and usually is held by more than one person. The most common type of joint or concurrent ownership is joint tenancy, which can exist between any two or more persons. Although joint tenants share a single title to the real estate, each owns an equal share of the whole.

5.   What are the essential elements of deed that will allow for a valid transfer of real estate?

ANSWER: All states have a law known as a statute of frauds requiring written transfers of real estate. Today, technical words are not needed in a deed, since any words that clearly show the grantor's intention to transfer are sufficient. There are eight essential elements of a modern deed: (1) Grantor's name, (2) Grantee's name, (3) Description of real estate to be conveyed, (4) Consideration, (5) Words of conveyance, (6) Signature of grantor, (7) Delivery and acceptances, (8) Proper execution.

6.   Identify the various means of mortgage foreclosure. Which exists in your state?

ANSWER: The four modern methods of foreclosure, depending on the law of a state, are: Judicial Proceeding, Power Of Sale, Strict Foreclosure, Entry And Possession.

CHAPTER 16

COMPLIANCE

OVERVIEW OF CHAPTER

As mentioned previously in the textbook, mortgage lending and the law are intertwined to a great extent. Throughout the 20th century, the Federal Government passed many laws, regulations or other requirements that impact all aspects of residential mortgage lending. As a result, mortgage lenders must be diligent in ensuring that they "lend legally". This chapter examines the basics of real estate and mortgage lending compliance. In class the Instructor should make sure that particular emphasis is placed on those laws and regulations pertaining to discrimination in real estate and mortgage lending. Emphasis should be placed on the understanding that if our society is going to work all people must believe they have an equal opportunity to obtain credit if they qualify.

The Instructor and the students should understand that changes are on-going in regards to compliance and the Instructor should be prepared to up-date the chapter's information with any changes as they occur. For example, as this Instructor's Manual is being written (September, 2003) major changes are being debated over changes to the *Real Estate Settlement Procedures Act* and the *Home Mortgage Disclosure Act*.

OBJECTIVES OF CHAPTER

Upon successful completion of this chapter, students should be able to:
- List the major rules and regulations impacting mortgage lending
- Discuss the nine prohibited bases of ECOA
- Discuss the usage of adverse action
- Understand the components of Annual Percentage Rate
- Explain how the Right to Rescind (Cancel) works
- Understand the recent law that applies to private mortgage insurance

OUTLINE OF CHAPTER

I.   Introduction

II.   Fair Lending

      A.   Fair Housing Act

      B.   Equal Credit Opportunities Act

III.   Truth-in-Lending

IV.   Real Estate Settlement Procedures Act

V.   Home Mortgage Disclosure Act

VI.   Fair Credit Reporting Act

VII.   Flood Disaster Protection Act

VIII.   Community Reinvestment Act

IX.   Fair Debt Collection Practices Act

X.   Home Equity Loan Consumer Protection Act

XI.   Homeowners Protection Act of 1998

SUGGESTED TRUE/FALSE QUIZ

1.   Fair Lending provisions come from the Equal Credit Opportunity Act solely.
F

2.   "Redlining" is the practice of some mortgage lenders to refuse to lend to Indians. **F**

3.   Whenever an applicant is turned down for a loan that person must receive a notice of adverse action. **T**

4.   The "effects test" applies when a practice that is not discriminatory on its face results in an adverse impact on protect4ed applicants. **T**

5.   The Equal Housing Poster only needs to be displayed in advertisements for mortgage loans. **F**

6. ECOA prohibits all discrimination tests or qualifications in mortgage lending. **F**

7. Truth-in-Lending applies to all mortgage loans. **F**

8. Mortgage lenders must ensure that flood insurance is in effect for the life of the loan. **T**

9. If an applicant(s) refuses to provide the government-monitoring information the lender must leave the space on the application blank. **F**

10. The Right to Rescind (Cancel) applies to all mortgage transactions. **F**

SUGGESTED SHORT ESSAY QUESTIONS

1. How did the passage of RESPA and subsequent amendments change loan application and closing procedures?

   ANSWER: RESPA required lenders to supply borrowers with information about settlement procedures, such as that contained in a booklet prepared by HUD, and a good faith estimate of settlement costs. This must be done within three days of receipt of the application, even though the loan might not be approved. Kickbacks for referring settlement business are prohibited. The law also placed limits on the amount of tax and insurance escrows a lender may require. HUD's Uniform Settlement Statement must be used at the closing.

2. What are the major federal regulations that are applicable to residential mortgage lending? Briefly describe their provisions.

   ANSWER: The major ones are:
   Truth-In-Lending, must supply applicant with annual percentage rate; provide applicant with TIL disclosure statement which discloses the finance charge, amount financed and the total of all payments

   Equal Credit Opportunities Act, lender may not discriminate on a prohibited basis, which means the "nifty nine" race, color, religion, national origin, sex, marital status, age, source of income, and reliance of consumer protection law.

   Fair Credit Report Act, applicant must be informed if their credit report contains adverse information.

   Flood Disaster Protection Act requires a lender to inform the applicant if property is in a flood area and require flood insurance if so located.

Real Estate Settlement Procedures Act requires lender to use the Uniform Settlement Statement, provide the Special Information Booklet to applicants, and provide a written estimate of settlement charges within 3 business days.

3.   List the circumstances under which ECOA permits questions concerning an applicant's spouse.

   ANSWER These questions are permitted when:
   1)   spouse will be contractually liable
   2)   spouse's income will be used to qualify
   3)   applicants live in a community property state
   4)   applicant will use child support, alimony, or maintenance payments from a spouse or former spouse to qualify.

ANSWERS TO ORAL DISCUSSION POINTS

The discussion points at the end of each chapter are intended for oral discussion in class. Suggested answers/points to emphasize for the questions are found below.

1.   ECOA (Regulation B) prohibits discrimination based upon what factors?

   ANSWER: 1. Sex, 2. Marital Status, 3. Age, 4. Race, 5. Color,   6. Religion, 7. National Origin, 8. Receipt of income from a public assistance program, 9. Good faith exercise of any right the applicant has under the Consumer Credit Protection act (or applicable state law).

2.   If a mortgage lender denies an application for a mortgage loan, what must the lender do? How is it done?

   ANSWER: Whenever a lender denies an application that lender must send a notice of adverse action to the applicant explaining why the application was denied.

3.   Are business loans covered by Truth In Lending? What is covered?

   ANSWER: Today TIL covers consumer purpose loans in amounts less than or equal to $25,000, or any consumer purpose loan, regardless of size, if secured by a 1 - 4 family dwelling or real property (e.g. vacant land). Business loans are NOT included in this regulation. Agricultural or loans to "non-natural persons" are NOT included in this regulation.

4.   What items are included in the Annual Percentage Rate? What is excluded?

ANSWER: The APR must include all Finance Charges - charges that are included in the Finance Charge: interest adjustments (odd days interest), loan discounts, origination fee,
mortgage insurance premiums, underwriting fee, fees for determining current tax lien status, fees for determining flood insurance requirements, borrower paid mortgage broker fees, any other service, transaction, activity or carrying charge. What is excluded is third party fees such as for appraisal, surveys, credit reports, etc.

5.   What is the Right of Rescission (Right to Cancel)? What is required of a mortgage lender?

ANSWER: TIL provides consumers with a very important right to cancel certain real estate financial transactions if they change their mind about wanting to put up their primary residence as security for a debt. At the closing of certain mortgage loans, a mortgage lender must give the "Notice of the Right of Rescission" (or as it is sometimes called, the right to cancel) to all parties with a legal interest in the property. The material disclosure must clearly state that the lender is taking a security interest in the applicant's principal residence (can be a mobile home or trailer), that the applicant has the right to cancel the transaction, how to cancel, the effects of canceling and the date the right to cancel expires.

6.   What is "life of loan coverage"? Why is this important to a mortgage lender?

ANSWER: Mortgage lender must ensure that flood insurance (if required at all) is in effect for the life of the loan. If property is later classified as in a special flood hazard area, lender must notify mortgagor of that fact and require flood insurance be purchased within 45 days and if flood insurance is not purchased within the 45 days, the lender must force place it. The importance to a lender of this requirement is to ensure that flood insurance exists.

CHAPTER 17
CONSTRUCTION LENDING

OVERVIEW OF CHAPTER

This chapter is new for this revised edition of the textbook. This new chapter was added to emphasize the importance of construction lending to the first mortgage loan process. Today it is common for a mortgage lender to commit to a construction loan and permanent financing at the same time and close both loans at one time. This chapter exposes the student to the special risks associated with this line of business and identifies the lenders that make these loans. The student will, upon completion of the chapter, understand the importance of construction lending to the entire economy.

Although the construction loan and permanent financing may be closed at the same time, the two loans are very different in their structure, the way funds are advanced and the risks to a lender. The basics of this loan are reviewed and the correct way to make these loans is examined.

OBJECTIVES OF CHAPTER

Upon successful completion of this chapter, students should be able to:

- Understand the importance of this loan to the entire economy.
- Explain which lenders make these loans and why they offer these loans.
- Discuss the process of advancing funds for a construction loan.
- Examine the similarities and differences between construction loans and permanent financing.
- Explain the process of originating a construction loan.

OUTLINE OF CHAPTER

I. Introduction to Construction Lending

    A. Housing starts

    B. Multiplier effect

SUGGESTED TRUE/FALSE QUIZ

1.   Over the past ten years the average number of new single-family housing starts has been approximately 1 million. **T**

2.   Construction lending is inherently different from permanent financing because of the way funds are disbursed. **T**

3.   The typical construction loan is for 90 days. **F**

4.   The most common method for closing construction loans is to close both the construction loan and the permanent loan at the same time. **T**

5.   The mechanic's lien in most states takes priority over the first mortgage – even if it is filed after loan closing of the first. **T**

6.   Appraisals for new construction are completed using plans and specifications. **T**

7.   If the applicant for a construction loan is the builder the mortgage lender will not require a credit check. **F**

8. Before issuing the final advance the construction lender must obtain a certificate of occupancy. **T**

9. Many lenders will not make a construction loan to a general contractor who will be the homeowner. **T**

10. All construction lenders can lend up to 95 percent of the cost of construction of a single-family home. **F**

MULTIPLE CHOICE QUESTIONS. More than one answer may be correct – select all correct answers. (Correct answers are italicized.)

1. Over the past ten years what has been the average annual starts for single-family construction?
   a. 200,000
   b. 500,000
   c. ***1,000,000***
   d. 2,000,000

2. The repayment of a construction loan is normally accomplished through:
   a. gift from a third party
   b. ***permanent financing***
   c. bonded indebtedness
   d. FHA loan

3. The amount of a construction loan is normally paid out:
   a. on an amortized basis
   b. in a lump sum upon completion of construction
   c. ***in stages based upon completion of construction - an advance***
   d. 50 percent upfront and 50 percent when finished

4. In almost all situations, the maximum loan to value for a construction loans is:
   a. 70 percent
   b. ***85 percent***
   c. 95 percent
   d. 100 percent

5.   Any person who performs work on a home and is not paid may file a:
   a.   mechanic's lien
   b.   contractor's lien
   c.   notice of cessation of labor
   d.   builder's lien

ANSWERS TO ORAL DISCUSSION POINTS

The discussion points at the end of each chapter are intended for oral discussion in class. Suggested answers/points to emphasize for the questions are found below.

1.   Why do lenders participate in residential construction lending?

   ANSWER: In order to earn a higher interest rate and provide excellent fee income which, given the short maturity of one year or less, is usually reflective of current market rates and results in a significantly higher yield than first mortgage lending. It also fills a product and market niche and reaches different segments within their marketing area, such as small builders and other individuals who will build the home. Finally it facilitates the expansion, renewal, and renovation of local housing stock. This increases the number and improves the condition of homes, which increases the market for mortgage loans and produces economic growth.

2.   How are construction loans structured?

   ANSWER: By establishing the value of the improvements and then advancing funds in step with progress of the construction. Term is brief – usually not over 12 months. Closing of the construction loan is often at the same time as the permanent financing.

3.   What are the benefits and drawbacks for both the lender and borrower in using a "two closing" loan products? A "one closing"?

   ANSWER: The two closing adds a repayment phase similar to permanent financing, with principal and interest amortization over a 15 to 30 year term. The borrower receives principal advances during the construction phase, but then the loan automatically converts to the permanent loan phase. The one closing alternative begins when the loan is fully advanced or at the end of the construction phase, again usually six to twelve months. The loan then repays with one balloon payment for the full outstanding balance and interest due at the end of construction or in one year, whichever occurs first.

4. How do construction loans differ from first mortgage, home improvement or home equity loans?

ANSWER; A construction loan is a short-term interim or temporary loan generally 6 to 12 months that is designed for construction purposes. A permanent loan (sometimes referred to as a take-out loan) is a long-term loan (15 to 30 years) and is the loan used to pay off the construction loan when construction is complete. Today, these loans are often closed at the same time and for the same interest rate. Home improvement and equity loans are usually second mortgages (either closed-end or revolving lines) used for specific home improvements purpose or other acceptable purposes.

5. What should a lender review when managing a construction loan portfolio?

ANSWER: The lender should be very concerned with the phases of disbursement of funds. Many construction lenders advance less than 20 percent of the total loan amount at closing, with additional funds disbursed later in the construction phase. After the borrower completes a stage of construction, the lender (or an agent) inspects the property, then disburses an amount that reflects the work completed. To avoid daily, small disbursements, the lender allows up to four or five construction advances.

CHAPTER 18

HOME EQUITY LOANS

OVERVIEW OF CHAPTER

This chapter is new for this revised edition of the textbook. This new chapter was added in recognition of the importance of equity loans to American homeowners and to mortgage lending in general. As mentioned in the text, nearly 30 percent of American homeowners currently have one of these loans. Most of the time these loans are used to fund education, home improvements, debt consolidation, etc., but they can also be a part of the total financing package used to purchase a home. The Instructor should be careful that the students understand that the type of equity loan discussed in this chapter does not include the over 100 percent loan-to-value equity loan made popular with TV ads.

During the first half of 2003 mortgage lenders were very aggressive in pricing equity loans – especially the variable-rate home equity line of credit (HELOC). The reason for this aggressive pricing was the desire on the part of the lenders to get homeowners to take one of these loans before rates began their expected increase. For that reason, the HELOC was often offered to homeowners at a rate that was below the prime rate. In addition, lenders were aggressive in pricing because they understood that these loans were very safe loans with low delinquency rates. After completing this chapter, students should understand why these loans perform so well and the reasons for the desirable performance.

The Instructor should ensure that the students understand the similarities and differences between the closed-end equity loan and the home equity line of credit. Many lenders treat these two loans as "siblings" i.e., underwrite them the same, use similar documentation (except for the note and security agreement) and provide similar incentives (such as no closing fees).

ERROR NOTE: On page 374 the historical example is incorrect for 1999, 2000 and 2001. The correct APR for those years should be: 1999 – 7.25 %; 2000 – 8.50 %; 2001 – 8.50 %.

OBJECTIVES OF CHAPTER

Upon successful completion of this chapter, students should be able to:

- Discuss the importance of this type of loan to the homeowner and to mortgage lenders.
- Understand the differences in documentation, processing, underwriting and closing between this type of loan and first mortgage loans.
- Be able to explain the difference in compliance for this type of loan and other mortgage loans.
- Explain why the home equity line of credit (HELOC) should be variable-rate.
- Provide examples of how the interest rate of a HELOC is calculated at and how it can change.
- Discuss the various methods for accessing a HELOC and which is the most rapidly growing way.
- Examine the most productive ways to market equity loans.

OUTLINE OF CHAPTER

I.   Introduction to Equity Loans.

    A.   Nomenclature

    B.   How important are equity loans to lenders?

    C.   Closing equity loans

    D.   Underwriting equity loans

    E.   Documentation

II.   Closed-end Second Mortgages

    A.   Fixed-rate product

    B.   Product design

III.   Home Equity Line of Credit

    A.   Index and margin

    B.   Introductory rate

C. Loan to value

D. Payment method

E. Adjustment periods

F. Methods of access

G. Title insurance or title search

H. Annual fee

I. Periodic statement

IV. Marketing Equity Loans

A. Marketing plan

B. Understand your market

C. Type of media used.

SUGGESTED TRUE/FALSE QUIZ

1. Approximately 30 percent of homeowners have an equity loan. **T**

2. An example of a common equity loan is a 125 % LTV loan. **F**

3. The average FICO score for an equity borrower is below 660. **F**

4. Most lenders used internal staff to close equity loans. **T**

5. Most equity lenders use the same processing and underwriting standards as for first mortgage loans. **F**

6. Most closed-end equity loans have a variable-rate. **F**

7. Both the closed-end equity loan and the home equity line of credit have a draw period and a repayment period. **F**

8. The interest rate on a HELOC is established by using an index and a margin. **T**

9. The most common repayment method for HELOCs today is similar to a self-amortizing first mortgage. **F**

10. A periodic statement is a Federal Reserve requirement for both equity loans. **F**

MULTIPLE CHOICE QUESTIONS. More than one answer may be correct – select all correct answers. (Correct answers are italicized.)

1. At the end of 2002 what percentage of homeowners had an equity loan?
   a. 10 percent
   b. 20 percent
   c. 30 percent
   d. 40 percent

2. Closed-end equity loans typically have the following characteristics:
   a. fixed-rate interest rate
   b. for a fixed term
   c. draw on a line of credit
   d. requires a separate draw and repayment period

3. Often home equity lines of credit have tiered rates. Features than can cause rates to vary include:
   a. type of collateral
   b. credit risk
   c. age of borrower
   d. location of property

4. The most common index for a HELOC is the:
   a. LIBOR
   b. six-month Treasury
   c. prime rate
   d. one-year T-bill

5. The most common repayment term for a HELOC is:
   a. amortized over life of loan
   b. interest only
   c. 1.5 percent of original loan
   d. based upon balance owed

ANSWERS TO ORAL DISCUSSION POINTS

The discussion points at the end of each chapter are intended for oral discussion in class. Suggested answers/points to emphasize for the questions are found below.

1.   Why are equity loans so popular with consumers?

      ANSWER: Equity loans are very popular with consumers for a number of reasons. Probably the most important reason is that the interest on the loan (with some limitations) can be deducted on a person's income tax. In fact, the modern equity loan market really began to thrive after the 1986 Tax Law change, which phased out the deduction of interest for consumer loans. Basically (with a few limitations), the interest of an equity loan up to $100,000 can be deducted as long as the loan does not exceed the original purchase price of the home.

2.   Identify and discuss the keys for success from a mortgage lender's perspective.

      ANSWER: Because the competition for equity loans is so intense, lenders must be aggressive in two areas if they want to attract consumers for their loans. The two keys to success for a lender's equity loans are product design and marketing. Product design refers to how the loan product is structured, including the interest rate and fees. Marketing simply means that lenders have to use as many means as practical to communicate to perspective borrowers why their equity loans are better than the competition. Both are equally important.

3.   What are the important differences between a closed-end equity loan and a home equity line of credit (HELOC)?

      ANSWER: The so-called traditional equity loan, often called a second mortgage, is a closed-end loan whereby the borrower is approved for a certain dollar amount that is advanced all at once and is repaid on an amortized basis over a fixed term. This loan is called closed-end because as payments are made those funds cannot automatically be borrowed again. The HELOC on the other hand is a revolving line of credit that if repaid during the draw period maybe borrowed again. It is a variable-rate loan with a separate draw and repayment period that is normally accessed by check.

4.   What is the most popular method of repaying a HELOC? Why is this payment method so popular?

      ANSWER: The vast majority of lenders (over 75 percent) today offer "interest only" payments. This "interest only" payment is, of course, used only during the draw period.

The reason so many lenders have converted to "interest only" is the substantial difference between an "interest only" payment and one that requires principal payments during the draw period.

5. What is the "Periodic Statement" that is used with HELOC? What information is contained in this statement?

ANSWER: Truth in Lending requires mortgage lenders with a HELOC product to send out a periodic statement to each HELOC borrower. Basically, the statement will look like the credit card statement many consumers receive in the mail each month.

- Balance outstanding at the beginning of the billing cycle,
- Identification of each credit transaction, including amount, date, etc.,
- Any credit to the account during the billing cycle including the amount and date,
- The periodic rate used to compute the finance charge, along with the range of balances to which it applies and the corresponding APR,
- Balance to which a periodic rate was applied,
- Amount of any finance charge added to an account during the billing cycle,
- APR equivalent to the total finance charge imposed during the billing cycle,
- Amounts, itemized and identified by type, of any charge other than finance charges debited to the account.